ZOE WAY NORTH AND SOUTH

AQUA AVE NORTH AND SOUTH

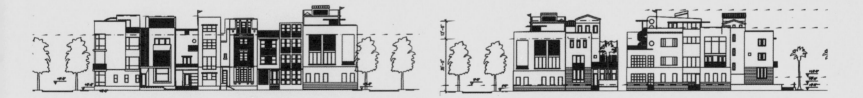

LAGUNA DRIVE WEST AND LAGUNA PATH SOUTH

AQUA
MIAMI MODERN BY THE SEA

AQUA

MIAMI MODERN BY THE SEA

BETH DUNLOP

Foreword by TERENCE RILEY　Photography by STEVEN BROOKE

Rizzoli

First published in the United States of America in 2007 by
RIZZOLI INTERNATIONAL PUBLICATIONS, INC.
300 Park Avenue South
New York, NY 10010
www.rizzoliusa.com

ISBN: 0-8478-2972-3
ISBN-13: 978-0-8478-2972-9
Library of Congress Control Number: 2007924259

Distributed to the U.S. trade by Random House, New York
Designed by Abigail Sturges
Printed and bound in China
2007 2008 2009 2010 2011/ 10 9 8 7 6 5 4 3 2 1

For Bill and Adam, and for those architects who saw there was
a better way to do it—and then did it—from whom I have
learned so much. —B.D.

For Suzanne and Miles, and with gratitude to Craig Robbins
for entrusting me with the documentation of his projects. —S.B.

CONTENTS

FOREWORD

Terence Riley

IN MY FIFTEEN YEARS of organizing exhibitions of architecture at the Museum of Modern Art in New York, the most commonly heard criticism of those shows was that the only thing missing was the architecture. The observation was not only obvious but true. Models, floor plans, elevations, perspective views, mock-ups, sample boards, and the like can, to the experienced viewer, provide many clues to the possible experience of architecture but always fall short of the actual thing: the sensation of experiencing a building or group of buildings in daylight as you pass through space and time.

Aqua at Allison Island is, to be sure, a real estate development. But it is also no less than Miami's most significant exhibition of contemporary architecture, full scale. In assembling a roster of local and national architectural talent to design the forty-six townhouses and three apartment blocks, Aqua's developer, Craig Robins, has demonstrated the reason that commerce and communication share the same linguistic root. While each of the living units represents a potential financial transaction, together they also represent an exchange of ideas about architecture, the city, and urban culture.

While there are some more immediate and local precedents for Robins's plan—such as the resort town of Seaside and the community of Celebration, both in Florida—the ultimate source for such an exhibition of architectural ideas is the 1927 Weissenhof Housing Colony undertaken in the city of Stuttgart, Germany. The project consisted of thirty-three buildings ranging from apartment blocks to row houses, duplexes and single-fam-

RIGHT An aerial image showing the southern tip of Allison Island.

ily homes designed by some of the most avant-garde architects of the day. With fully outfitted interiors, the Weissenhof Housing Colony provided an often skeptical public with a full-scale demonstration of the advantages of modern architecture at a time when traditionally designed and built houses were still the norm. The project offered a demonstration of not only new architectural forms and spaces, but new materials, new technologies, and bold proposals for new ways of living.

The architects at Aqua were not challenged by the same heavy brief—the Weissenhof architects were not only expected to create new paradigms for living, they were supposed to make the results low-cost as well—but broke new ground in other ways. The word "design" is often overused, if not abused, in most real estate marketing, appearing as one of many items on a list of amenities that are more commodities than anything that might be considered an idea. Aqua tries to move design to center stage in the conception of its development.

Also, Aqua displays more comfort with the realities of contemporary urban life than Seaside or Celebration, combining high-rise living with a range of more traditional townhouse designs, much as you would find in virtually any city in the country. In contrast to such "communities" as Nantucket, whose picture-perfect image is enforced by myriad regulations, Aqua appears as less a fantasy than a thoughtful exploration of how diversity enhances a community.

INTRODUCTION

THE STUCCO BUILDINGS, painted subtly and accented engagingly, glint in the sunlight. They are clearly modern but somehow seem to have come from a century's worth of Modernism, not just the recent past. Densely aggregated, the rows of tall townhouses are familiar and yet mysterious: ever so reminiscently European but also definitively American; of another era yet firmly rooted in ours.

Though it is tucked behind a stylized gatehouse, Aqua is not hidden from view; much to the contrary, one can see it quite clearly from any number of vantage points. Yet to see it fully—to understand its details, its aesthetic, its emerging idiosyncrasies (in any neighborhood, this is a positive quality, not a negative one)—one must see Aqua close-up and on foot. At that point it becomes impossible to dismiss Aqua as just another speculative, exclusive development. It has neither the thinness, the tinniness, nor the superficiality that one so often associates with speculation. Indeed, Aqua's developer, Craig Robins, had an overriding goal that as much as possible, the architecture look "handmade." In an affirmation of city life, Aqua has become an exemplar model for urban infill building, and most important, posits an alternative to the ubiquitous high rise.

Aqua sits on the southerly tip of a small island in the middle of a waterway in Miami Beach. In the short history of the New Urbanism—the movement that has built and rebuilt neighborhoods, suburban communities, and towns with an eye to scale, amenity, visual pleasure, an understanding of history, and much more—this is the first to be predicated on what one might call modern historicism. Its buildings reflect a century of

RIGHT The Aqua plan shows the layout of streets and the placement of the buildings.

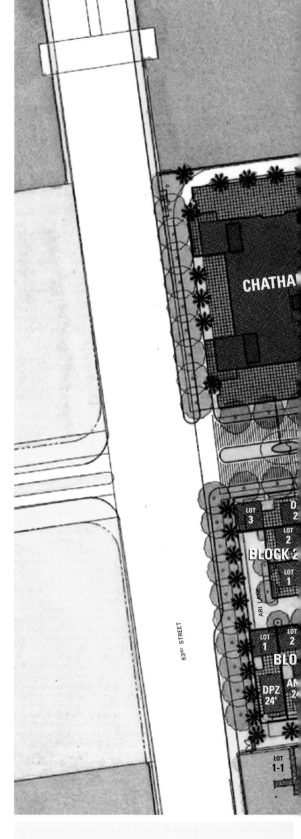

SPEAR

GORLIN

INDIAN CREEK

LOT 12-10

LOT 11-10

LOT 10-10

LOT 9-10

AQUA WALK

AQUA STREET

BDA 30'

BDA 24'

DPZ 24'

BLOCK 10

BDA 30'

LOT 9

LOT 12

LOT 11

LOT 10

LOT 8

ASA 36'

LOT 7

AGA 30'

HHA 30'

SMA 30'

LOT 4

LOT 6

HHA 30'

LOT 5

BLOCK 8

WCA 30'

LOT 1

BLOCK 10

SMA 30'

BDA 24'

BLOCK 6

LOT 4

AGA 30'

BLOCK 9

EFM 30'

LOT 2

AGA 30'

AMA 24'

LOT 3

LOT 2

LOT 2

WCA 30'

LOT 5

BDA 24'

LOT 2

LOT 1

ASA 36'

AQUA STREET

DPZ 30'

LOT 1

LOT 4

DPZ 30'

LOT 3

BDA 30'

BLOCK 5

SMA 36'

LOT 2

LOT 1

BLOCK 10

SMA 36'

BLOCK 3

DPZ 30'

LOT 3

AMA 24'

LOT 5

SMA 36'

LOT 5

ASA 36

EFM 30'

LOT 2

LOT 2

EFM 30'

LOT 6

DPZ 30'

LOT 1

LOT 4

BLOCK 7

LOT 1

LOT 2

ARI WAY

LOT 5

LOT 3

SMA 30'

WCA 30'

LOT 2

LOT 1

LOT 3

LOT 4

BDA 30'

HHA 30'

AMA 24'

BDA 24'

LOT 1

BLOCK 4

LAGUNA WALK SOUTH

LOT 3-10

SMA 36'

BDA 24'

AMA 24'

ASA 36'

LAGUNA DRIVE WEST

LOT 2-10

LOT 1-10

LOT 6-7

LOT 5-7

LOT 4-7

LOT 3-7

LOT 2-7

LOT 1-7

WALK NORTH

LOT 1-4

LOT 2-4

LOT 3-4

LOT 4-4

LOT 5-4

N

AQUA
Allison Island

a.net

Dacra

10.09.03

15

architectural evolution and change, but they do so seamlessly, and not at all self-consciously. Though inspired by and built in the tradition of the New Urbanism, this affluent, gated enclave of expensive houses and apartments does not adhere to the strict definition of the term.

On August 16, 2005, the *Harvard Design Magazine* hosted a small symposium at Aqua. In attendance were Robins; Aqua's designer, Elizabeth Plater-Zyberk; Harvard Professor Alex Krieger; and others.[1] The group toured Aqua's forty-six townhouses and three midrise apartment buildings, examining the urban plan, the streetscape, and the architecture. The buildings at Aqua are designed by ten different architects, some of them quite renowned and others little known, purposefully so. Each of the ten worked within the formal guidelines of an elegant plan developed by Duany Plater-Zyberk & Company, or DPZ as it is generally known.

Aqua sits on eight-and-a-half acres of Allison Island in the northerly part of Miami Beach. In all, there are one hundred and five units. It is an urban residential enclave that is intended to embrace its tropical setting. The goals at Aqua were many: to create an aesthetically harmonious neighborhood with buildings that reflect Miami Beach's historic twentieth-century architecture; also to celebrate the traditions of urbanism and prove that good urban design can lead to good architecture that offers its residents both a public life and the opportunity for privacy. "You have built a jewel here," said Krieger, after pondering the issues for the several hours of the Harvard seminar. "You are in a city in a very divergent, diverse context, and this is a part of it, as opposed to a place apart."[2]

Allison Island sits in the middle of Indian Creek, which branches off from Biscayne Bay and runs parallel to the Atlantic Ocean for some six

miles. In the earliest days of settlement, it was not an island, but rather a place of enormous fascination, a "crocodile hole" deep in the mangroves that rose out of the water in a thick tangle. On July 10, 1924, the *Miami Daily News* announced that "the dredge Norman Davis of the Clark Dredging Co. is completing the filling of Allison Island." The newspaper reported that the island would be five hundred feet wide and eight thousand five hundred feet long. It would be divided north and south by a drawbridge so that "large boats will have a passage through Indian Creek. Plans are being drawn and a permit from the war department has been obtained."[3]

Today, along this route—in a scull, kayak, or fancier pleasure boat— one can find examples of most eras of Miami Beach's architecture, as well as most types, including hotels and condominiums, modest early mod-ernist apartments and motels, a bit of Art Deco (though most of that is in the southern end of the city), and lavish Mediterranean houses.

Like much of Miami Beach, Allison Island is a product of entrepreneur Carl Fisher's vast imagination and named for Fisher's close friend, James Allison. The two men had founded the Prest-o-Lite corporation, which manufactured and held the patent to the compressed gas headlamp, a requisite for the automobile industry. By 1913 Prest-o-Lite was doing so well that Allison and Fisher sold it to the Union Carbide Corporation for the then-whopping sum of nine million dollars. The two men, along with other partners, had also developed the Indianapolis Motor Speedway.

Fisher also built, in 1913, the east-west Lincoln Highway from New York to San Francisco and a year later, the Dixie Highway, which went at that time from Indianapolis to Miami, where he and his wife, Jane, had pur-

chased a house on Brickell Avenue in 1910. Fisher had invested $50,000 in the completion of the first bridge linking Miami Beach to the mainland; his (and ultimately, the city's) future was set.

In exchange for his assistance, John Collins—who himself had come to Miami Beach when it was little more than a few residences, sand, and scrub—deeded Fisher much of the center portion of what would become Miami Beach. Fisher in turn set about developing it, a task that included a fair amount of dredge and fill to create islands, among them Allison Island. In due course, Fisher lured his friend Allison to Florida.

While Fisher was promoting Miami Beach with his full resources, Allison's interest was more limited. He built an aquarium at Fifth Street and Biscayne Bay—now high-rise condominiums—and on the island that bore his name built Allison Hospital, after his convalescence from a heart attack in a then-unappealing hospital in Fort Lauderdale. Fisher and Allison were businessmen more than idealists, so one can speculate that a hospital luring convalescents from the north must have seemed potentially lucrative. "Between the place where the bridge crosses the island and

the southern portion of the island will be the sanitarium to be built by James A. Allison and the Fisher Properties, announcement of which was made two weeks ago," reported the *Miami Daily News* which also said that the hospital "will be a most ideal place for an institution of this kind as it will be off by itself where it is quiet and yet where friends and relatives of the sick can find places to stay."[4]

The hospital operated under that title between January 1, 1926, when it first opened its doors, and 1927, when it was taken over by the Catholic Church and ultimately by the Franciscan Sisters of Allegany, thus the new name St. Francis Hospital. At its closing in the 1990s, *The Miami Herald* reported that it had been built at a cost of $3,652,000, adding that "the hospital was known for its state-of-the-art facilities and lavish care—a French chef cooked patient meals and every room had electric fans."[5] The hospital prospered and grew; in 1964 three acres of fill were added to the five and a half it already occupied. A parking garage, with three stories of offices above, was built, and the original, rather glamorous Mediterranean

Revival building was updated, added to, and altered quite significantly. St. Francis held its prominence as part of the Miami Beach medical establishment until the early 1980s, when demographics shifted and other hospitals began to compete for both doctors and patients. In 1993 the facility was purchased by the Columbia Healthcare System, and the name was changed to Miami Beach Community Hospital. Within two years, St. Francis Hospital had closed down for good and was put up for sale. The land was optioned more than once, but each time the sale fell through because the prospective owners—including one who wished to put an Alzheimer's care facility on the island—could not work through an acceptable zoning plan. Eventually, the land and buildings were sold to Craig Robins for twelve million dollars. Thus began chapter two in the man-made island's history.

In many ways, the story of Aqua is the story of Robins, the developer, as it encapsulates much of what he learned in the first four decades of his life: the architecture he grew up with, the ideas of design and urbanism

he learned to embrace, the art that he both loved and collected. Robins was born in 1963 at St. Francis Hospital—a poetic punctuation point in the saga—and grew up not ten miles away on Miami Beach's Star Island. Later, he went to the University of Michigan, spent a formative year studying in Spain, and then attended law school at the University of Miami. Like others in his generation—the first to do so—he returned to Miami Beach. He had a feeling for the cosmopolitan urban life, honed by his studies in Europe, and a love for art. Robins was immediately attracted to the still-emerging South Beach, with its candy-hued buildings. He was still studying for the bar exam, but he found himself drawn to development, especially in South Beach. In the late 1980s, South Beach was just beginning to emerge from decades of doldrums and was doing so with a burst of creativity. The district's more than eight hundred historic buildings—most of which were built in the late 1930s and early 1940s in a whimsical tropical Art Deco style—were being repaired, renovated, and painted in a blaze of pastel colors that gave rise to even further creativity.

It was the right moment to step into the Beach's preservation scene; the wildly popular television series, *Miami Vice*, had begun its all-on-location filming in 1984 (and would last for five seasons until the spring of 1990), bringing with it producer Michael Mann's famous (and city-shaping) edict for locations, which was "no earth tones." Robins's first two projects were buildings bought in 1987 with another developer, Tony Goldman. Then came such projects as the renovations of the Webster and Marlin hotels on Collins Avenue. He also brought with him several partners, his stepbrother, Scott Robins, and the founder of the Jamaica-based Island Records, Chris Blackwell, who—among other things—is known for launching the careers of such musicians as Bob Marley, U2, Steve Winwood, Melissa Etheridge, and the Cranberries. For the Marlin, Robins hired two emerging Miami artists, Jens Diercks (whose work involves dismantling and reassembling furniture as art) and Gary Feinberg (a painter with an array of interests), to create a version of a Jamaican cook shack. The result was ShaBeen's Cookshack and Bar, which looked paint-splattered and jerrybuilt, but was actually a carefully calculated work of art.

Robins's first South Beach venture had been the creation of a studio for the brilliant artist Carlos Alfonzo.[6] Robins also in that period commissioned the Spanish artist Antoni Miralda to create a canopy for the otherwise bleak 1960s building on Washington Avenue. He housed a number of Miami's emerging artists, among them Carlos Alfonzo, Jose Bedia, Craig Coleman, Roberto Juarez, Kenny Scharf, and the architect Carlos Zapata. He brought in the New York artist Keith Haring to open a Pop Shop. For Robins, the development of South Beach was not just about commissioning and sheltering artists, it was about the creation of style. In essence, he was taking what were stylized works of architecture and transforming them into stylish destinations. It was not the trend in real estate at the time; indeed, throughout the country, the 1980s saw little invention in urban architecture. The period was characterized by an outpouring of corporate Modernism. Style and design were not on the table, except perhaps as points of discussion. South Beach offered a different opportunity in that it was at the time wildly undervalued and thoroughly underestimated—except by a few—and yet filled with disarming 1930s and 1940s architecture.

RIGHT A view of Laguna
Drive West showing the
docks leading to the townhouses.

And indeed, the Miami of the 1980s was far enough off the radar that it offered opportunities for new and experimental thinking. Arquitectonica had come onto the scene with its bold, brash, colorful towers, and the Art Deco District was being rediscovered thanks largely to the efforts of Barbara Capitman. An architectural scheme created under the auspices of the architect Charles Harrison Pawley and executed by the designer Leonard Horowitz had brought bright pastel colors into the fledgling National Historic District. Robins took it a step further, commissioning artists such as Kenny Scharf and Roberto Juarez, in addition to Miralda, Feinberg, and Diercks, to add to or interpret the historic architecture.[7]

Robins simultaneously began to collect art. He began buying pieces by the Los Angeles–based artist John Baldessari, whose primary works are photo-collages and who has been the subject of more than 120 solo exhibitions in his lifetime. Robins refers to Baldessari as "the artist I have collected most in depth; not only have I been inspired by him but I have learned so much about art from him directly and more so from collecting his work." His collection now is wide ranging but includes works by, among others, Kai Althoff, Marlene Dumas, Guillermo Kuitca, Paul McCarthy, and Richard Tuttle. At one point Robins said, almost parenthetically, that his favorite artist is Goya, and indeed he has been able to purchase some first edition prints.

In architecture, likewise, he sought the unusual and patronized emerging talent, including Patty Barrocas, Anabel Hoffman, Mark Hoffman, Juan Lescano, Derrick Smith, Trelles Architects (Luis and Jorge Trelles and Maritere Cabarrocas-Trelles), and Carlos Zapata. He also—in conjunction with business partner Blackwell—hired the Polish-born but London-bred designer Barbara Hulanicki, who had gained fame in the 1960s with her store Biba. Later, Robins would point to Blackwell as having had a "transformative" influence, showing him that one could indeed approach business as "creativity" and in the doing, not limit it to art and design.[8]

This was a critical juncture: Robins began seeing the city not just as a blank canvas but also as an empty stage, creating the context for architecture, art, and design, and then producing events that celebrated all three. With his stepbrother, Robins had bought the northern half of Espanola Way, a quaint, Spanish-styled enclave built as an artists' colony in the 1920s that still remained within the Art Deco District. DACRA, Robins's real estate development company, renovated the buildings it bought—most of the south side of the street was in the single ownership of Linda Polansky—and set about returning it to its origins as an art center. Almost simultaneously, Robins began to program the street, bringing in such events as an outdoor flamenco performance by Joaquin Cortes, which was an ode to the impact Barcelona had made on him years earlier. But it also reflected what his ventures could embrace: that real estate could be celebrated as architecture; that the architecture could in turn create urbanism but at the same time provide a context for art; and that architecture can provide a stage for many other forms of creativity, from the design arts to the fine arts to the performing arts.

In the course of his South Beach development period (the 1980s and 1990s), Robins began to explore the ideas of New Urbanism, as well. He traveled to Seaside several times with Andrés Duany (on one trip, he was also accompanied by Nicholas Pritzker, now chairman and chief executive officer of the Hyatt Development Corporation, and hotelier Ian Schrager), and began talking with Duany and Elizabeth Plater-Zyberk in an effort to learn the economics, development strategies, and impact of the New Urbanist movement. Robins came to the New Urbanism from his own (and Miami Beach's) unique development model in historic preservation, one that, in terms of urbanism, closely presages the New Urbanist model.

By the mid-1990s, Robins had moved from his work in South Beach to the long-beleaguered Miami Design District across Biscayne Bay in the city of Miami. There he had begun buying large—and largely unused—furniture showrooms, including the exquisite 1926 Mediterranean Moore Furniture building and a number of architecturally undistinguished warehouses and showrooms. He soon acquired enough real estate to make a critical mass and set about applying the lessons he'd learned both from South Beach and in his more recent studies of the New Urbanism. Eventually, he convinced the City of Miami to join with him in hiring Plater-Zyberk to do a master plan for the neighborhood, and an intensive time-constrained workshop known as a charrette followed. The charrette brought in a number of local architects, planners, designers, landscape architects, civic and community activists, and others, resulting in a plan with a fairly rigorous landscape component and specific strategies for bringing more pedestrian life into the long-dormant district. To renovate and adapt the Design District's buildings, Robins hired a number of architects, among them Alison Spear, who had moved her primary practice from

New York to the Design District; Walter Chatham of New York; Terrence Riley, then curator of architecture at the Museum of Modern Art in New York (and, as of 2006, director of the Miami Art Museum); as well as Derrick Smith, Anabel Delgado, and Patty Barrocas, all of whom had been involved in Robins's Miami Beach ventures. Somewhat later, he commissioned two young, husband-and-wife architectural firms, Penabad and Cure, and Khoury-Vogt, to design two side-by-side new buildings and a plaza in the heart of the district. Robins also commissioned a number of large-scale works of art. The widely exhibited Cuban-born Jose Bedia did murals for the Buick Building, and on a street corner, the public artists Roberto Behar and Rosario Marquardt created an outdoor plaza entitled *The Living Room*. An initial Behar and Marquardt project, a mural for the Design District's Buick Building, was short-lived, in part because the paint did not stand up to the harsh environment of the blazing sun and fierce tropical rains. Robins installed Miralda's giant, mirror-tiled, wooden high-heeled shoe (officially entitled *Gondola Shoe*) in the atrium of his Melin Building. It was just as his aspirations for the Design District were beginning to come to fruition that Robins was able to buy the St. Francis Hospital site.

Though he had a fundamental idea that he would create something of value with the land, he had no specific plans; however, based on his trips to New Urbanist sites and his existing collaboration with Plater-Zyberk, the prospect of a lower-scale, pedestrian-oriented development was enticing. Robins wanted to do a project that would be modern, in part to prove that the New Urbanism was not inextricably tied up with style, and in part because he wanted Aqua to pay homage to the architecture he had grown up with—not just Miami Beach's Art Deco buildings but also the early postwar modern resort designs that ranged from such lavish (in scale and style) Morris Lapidus hotels as the Fontainebleau, Eden Roc, or Americana, to modest motels and apartment complexes that had been built in Miami Beach (and throughout South Florida) in such abundance. The latter was a new typology for the postwar era, often intended to lure the passing motorist and certainly—in such warm-climate locales as Miami or Los Angeles—aimed at capturing the climate with breezeways and single-loaded corridors. While Lapidus became more or less legendary for his hotels, a cadre of other influential architects—among them Gilbert Fein, Norman Giller, Melvin Grossman, and and Igor Polevitzky—were active in that immediate postwar era, influenced largely by the European prototypes of the Bauhaus.[9] It is still possible, in some contiguous blocks of Miami Beach, to see groupings of these buildings as one growing up in the 1960s or 1970s might have.

To look at this area chronologically, one must start with Art Deco. Miami Beach's Art Deco District is unique in America for many reasons. It is essentially one mile square, and within that narrow geographical confine can be found, still standing today, nearly eight hundred low-rise stucco buildings in the Art Deco style, which emanated from the Exposition Internationale des Arts Décoratifs et Industriels held in Paris in 1925 and was adapted in architecture, first in urban skyscrapers, and then in lower-scaled resorts. In Miami Beach, Art Deco took a specific form—one that can also be seen in seaside resorts elsewhere in the world including Antibes in France and Haifa, Israel, though not in this concentration. It is a stucco Deco style, simple and even rudimentary, with enormous reliance on geometry and limited decoration. The Art Deco buildings of Miami Beach are noteworthy for both their vertical thrust and horizontality, and for the tension between the two. They are also jaunty, lighthearted buildings with any number of nautical allusions—pipe rails, porthole windows—and whimsical finials and spires. Of particular note are the climatic adaptations—cross-ventilation, cantilevered overhangs, and "eyebrows" to shade windows. They are also buildings that express an architecture of optimism; built in the height of the Depression, these are buoyant, joyous buildings with architecture that rose out of adversity to express a faith in the future.

Most important, these are structures best seen in aggregate, as a composition of a larger whole. With some eight hundred such buildings clustered within a single square mile, the impact is powerful; few of the buildings would be architectural stars on their own, but taken together they are a sight to behold. Significantly, the Miami Beach's Art Deco District became the country's first modern National Historic District: at the time, in 1978, the youngest ever, in terms of the age of the buildings.

Many of the aesthetic and structural considerations of Miami Beach's Art Deco buildings carried over into the new designs of the immediate postwar period. These are buildings that in many ways are particular to Miami, to Miami Beach even, in that though they are modern and clearly differentiated from the generally smaller and more whimsical buildings in the Art Deco style. They are nonetheless masonry buildings, concrete and stucco, which means that the modernist language is far more limited, more specific to climate and geography than it might otherwise have been. Unlike in the rest of the country, there are few glass curtain walls to be found in the midcentury hotels and apartment complexes of Miami Beach.

By the end of World War II, many of the major figures in architecture—among them Mies van der Rohe, Marcel Breuer, and Walter Gropius—had emigrated from Europe to America, bringing with them the International Style. Philip Johnson, who as director of the department of architecture at

the Museum of Modern Art, had completed his own later-in-life architecture degree at Harvard and was just starting to build. Yet for all its influence, the Miesian style that emanated from the Bauhaus did not have as much impact on Miami as one might have expected. (Arguably the work of Le Corbusier, which was more tropical, somehow more adaptable, and better suited for the climate, did.) Instead, what emerged, particularly in postwar Miami Beach, is what one might call an evolutionary American Modernism, buildings that seamlessly evolved from Art Deco, stripping away the details and slowly incorporated the International Style. If anything, the kinship was stronger to the later works of such architects as Ely Jacques Kahn[10] or Raymond Hood, whose work likewise evolved from Art Deco Moderne into a more pure form of Modernism.

As a side note, the emerging idea of multiple modernisms is truly applicable in Florida, where neither one singular approach nor the Miesian aesthetic took firm hold. Starting in the years after the war, Paul Rudolph was starting to make an impact with his work in Sarasota, and elsewhere throughout the state, architects were experimenting with small suburban houses and other projects that derived, essentially, from Frank Lloyd Wright and Richard Neutra as much as Mies. Daring and often fairly fragile, these houses explored structure and nature simultaneously, but they were most often tucked away amid greenery in suburban or even rural areas and not part of the larger cultural landscape that was postwar tourist Miami Beach.

A close examination of such buildings as the Seville, the Carillon, the Sherry Frontenac, and the Deauville shows their role in setting the precedent for Aqua's three midrise apartment buildings, not just in scale and material but also in capturing the essentially buoyant and optimistic feel of those postwar works. Even in the growing sophistication of the late 1940s and 1950s, Miami Beach's architecture always remained a resort architecture with all that implied, be it a swoop at a rooftop or a whimsical entrance canopy. Most prominent in the era, of course, was the architect Morris Lapidus, who in such works as the Fontainebleau, the Eden Roc, and the Americana employed the International Style—filtered through many lenses, including Oscar Niemeyer's in Brazil. Lapidus gave Miami Beach a new signature style that was double-edged. At the base came the building, and Lapidus designed a good building usually; then came his signature styling that ranged from Jetson-like architectural interventions he would call woggles or cheese holes, to more elaborate stage settings, such as stairs to nowhere that hotel guests could use for grand lobby entrances.

Of course, this postwar architecture in Miami Beach was aimed at resort living, at midrise hotels along the beach, or at housing newly returned soldiers and their families, who happily filled the new two-story apartments in the northerly end of Miami Beach—simple stucco buildings with single-loaded outdoor corridors, often with a single flourish of a staircase or porte cochère. Likewise, the newly mobile vacationers began to arrive by automobile to check into similarly designed motels that lined the highway and, in places, the waterfront.

Like the Art Deco architecture of the prewar period, this too was more dependent on the aggregate of the whole—the sum of the parts—than on single major landmarks. The compositions were dependent on rhythmic relationships, at the small scale of window to wall and at the larger scale of building to building.

Importantly, it is the architecture of these decades, essentially the 1930s through the 1950s, that informed the stylistic considerations of Aqua. For some of Aqua's ten architects it was a direct influence; for others it was subliminal. Alison Spear, for example, grew up in Miami in a design-aware family, which makes her eponymous Spear Building at Aqua directly referential. Suzanne Martinson and Adolfo Albaisa, too, were Miami-born and in many ways informed by the architecture that shaped their early years. For others, the work derived from observation and analysis, not just of the existing body of modernist architecture but also of the climate, culture, horticulture. Still others operated more subliminally, extrapolating and interpreting.

Robins not only grew up with the compelling, if long underappreciated, resort architecture of Miami Beach, but he also had become a student of

the New Urbanism, both during his trips and in the course of conversations and charrettes with Duany and Plater-Zyberk. At Aqua, Robins was less interested in the kind of project that Seaside represented—in part out of pragmatics, in that he was working with approximately one-tenth as much land and restrictive zoning—and more interested in the potential of New Urbanism to create new infill urban neighborhoods and restore life to existing city districts. He was also intrigued by the challenge of working within the confines of the New Urbanism while embracing a modernist aesthetic, to prove that the ideas were not inextricably bound in the kind of stylistic predilections it is often criticized for, even if the use of historicist styles often flows organically from the process of creating towns and neighborhoods that have a more seamless fit with their surroundings and create the kind of instant urbanism that otherwise can take decades to achieve. Of course that worked to an advantage in Aqua's case, where invoking the architectural history of Miami Beach meant invoking Mod-

ernism from the middle years of the twentieth century. Further, Robins knew he wanted Aqua to seem "handmade"—a difficult challenge with speculative housing that has to be constructed economically—and thus wanted to employ many of the design strategies and building techniques that have successfully given some New Urbanist communities a quality of being older and more entrenched than they were chronologically.

Other driving forces behind Aqua were those threads that began to emerge in Robins's early days in South Beach, the ideas of interweaving art, design, and architecture into what was essentially a real estate venture. "The client looms large in this story," said Plater-Zyberk.[11] Indeed, the two—the developer and the town planner—were well matched in this. Both are progressive, integrated thinkers. Both can capture the biggest picture and yet understand the fine-tuned details. Both look at the existing world and seek insights and new ideas from the already built. Robins is more restless, more interested in new ideas; Plater-Zyberk is more rooted, finding her insights in the existing environment. In this case, they did not have to look far for either.

An initial and all-embracing goal for the project was a blunt one, to take the garishishness out of the architecture and mediate between the high-rise district and the historic and affluent single-family neighborhoods of Miami Beach. The northern half of Alison Island (it is dissected by one of the two major through-roads in Miami Beach) remained an enclave of single-family residential buildings, as did the affluent Miami Beach neighborhood to the west. To the east, however, the land had been slowly filling with new high-rises, hemming Allison Island in visually. These were not handsome structures either, each new one somehow more garish than the last.

An early step was bringing the nearby residents to agreement with the project, a tricky proposition in an already traffic-plagued neighborhood, even though the driving idea of creating a midrise buffer zone was compelling in its intelligence. In the course of a number of meetings, Robins and Plater-Zyberk carved out an acceptable zoning package with the residents, which—despite its moments of acrimony, which are of course typical in any work with neighborhoods—came to a felicitous conclusion. The first sketches show the way in which the zoning package, and in fact the overall building envelope and site plan, evolved during discussions with the nearby residents. By May 1999 Robins had achieved Miami Beach Planning Board approval for the island's rezoning from a narrow hospital use to a multi-family planned residential category, thus setting the stage for the future.

Plater-Zyberk is not only with her husband, Duany, a principal in their eponymous architecture and town planning firm, but is also dean of the University of Miami School of Architecture. After her education at Princeton and Yale universities, Plater-Zyberk joined with Duany and three other partners (Bernardo Fort-Brescia, Laurinda Spear, and Hervin Romney) to found the architectural firm Arquitectonica; however, in 1989 Plater-Zyberk and Duany broke off to form their own firm, taking with them just one client who would shape their future. That was Robert Davis, the developer of Seaside. For them, it was life-shaping, as Seaside spelled a sea change in town planning, laying the groundwork for the development of the New Urbanism.

Over the years, DPZ grew enormously in scope and stature. By the time Aqua was envisioned, the firm was responsible for hundreds of new town designs and a number of important planning studies in Miami and elsewhere. The firm's preferred planning methodology, the charrette, had become almost normative in Miami, and indeed across the country. And the successes of their work were there to be seen. Without the already long-standing relationship, it might have been more difficult for Robins to persuade DPZ to take on a small luxury housing project, even despite his larger ambitions for it.

In the initial stages, DPZ thought about saving and somehow transforming the hospital building; ultimately only the most recent structure, the parking garage built in the 1960s, could be saved. The plan evolved. An early and central decision was made to opt for a more picturesque plan in which the dramatic views into Indian Creek would unfold slowly, which would make the water, in Plater-Zyberk's words, "a destination, part of an itinerary." Aqua's project manager, Ludwig Fontalvo-Abello, shepherded the design into development, and the development into architecture; he reflected that most DPZ projects rely on "skinny streets" to weave a tight web of urbanism. In Aqua, however, the streets flare to maximize the perspectives, the views.[12]

Another critical decision was what might best be called "car capture," in which most of the cars entering the project would be sent immediately to the garage, leaving the streets uncongested. Rather than building more conventionally with swimming pools in abundance, only two were designed, one in the midst of the midrise towers and the other at the island's tip, allowing all residents to share in the most spectacular vistas to the south, east, and west.

The plan evolved and changed. At one point, a fourth eight-story apartment building was contemplated but abandoned in favor of more townhouses and thus more streetscape. An ideal of the New Urbanism is of course mixed-use development, but in meetings with the neighbors it was made abundantly clear that the mixed-use approach was not popular. The code was written by the attorney Santiago Echimendia. DPZ polished the plan, which basically relied on three midrise apartment buildings facing the high-rise condominiums to the east, with a loop road running in front of them to the tip of the island and back out along the water's edge to the west, framing three small blocks of townhouses.

A wish list of architects was drawn up. Though the selection of the architects loomed large, both in the concept of Aqua and its eventual execution, Robins later reflected that the development was "never an architecturally driven project, but rather a project driven by urban design."[13] The New York architect Walter Chatham, who had collaborated on several projects in the Design District and had renovated Robins's own house, opted for the most visible but the toughest job, that of renovating the parking garage and adapting the upper floors into apartments. Chatham had been an early investor in Seaside, where he'd built a cot-

FACING PAGE
The narrowness of the island
allowed Duany Plater-Zyberk
& Company to establish a
visual hierarchy.

tage for his family; at the time (and to date, in fact) it was one of the more daring designs in Seaside, based on the Southern prototype "shotgun shack" and eschewing any of the more sentimental attributes of most houses there. It received both attention and awards.

Chatham was reared in Washington D.C. and educated at the University of Maryland; in the course of his education, he took a year off to work at the then-fledgling firm of Arquitectonica when Duany and Plater-Zyberk were still partners with Laurinda Spear, Fort-Brescia, and Romney. Chatham went on, in New York, to cofound the firm of 1100 Architect, then set off on his own. An early project was the house for Seaside, which focused attention on him, as did a Caribbean beach house he designed for his father-in-law. Chatham also enjoyed a certain celebrity as the architect for two Manhattan apartments for Martha Stewart and one for her daughter, Alexis.

Alison Spear, whose practice is based both in Miami and New York, had been involved in Aqua from the earliest days and was selected to design the first of the two all-new midrise buildings, which has sixty units. A Miamian, Spear was educated at both Cornell and Columbia universities; she opened her own office in New York specializing in interiors, which set her apart from her already established sister, Laurinda Spear, who had not only cofounded Arquitectonica but who, with her husband, Bernardo Fort-Brescia, had turned the firm into one with a widespread international clientele for commercial and institutional buildings. Alison Spear, on the other hand, gained considerable renown for her vital, well-wrought, sophisticated interiors, working both as an architect and an interior designer. By the late 1990s, she moved her office to the Miami Design District, while keeping the New York practice. She had collaborated with Robins on the award-winning Holly Hunt Showroom in his Buick Building.

The third apartment block had not been on the original plans, but DPZ ultimately determined the need for two separate buildings along the west side of the island. For this one, the New York architect Alexander Gorlin was chosen. The Yale-trained Gorlin opened his own practice in 1987 after winning the Rome Prize in Architecture and since has emerged as a thoughtful modernist. He is also the author of two books on townhouse design. That he was the third architect selected for the multi-family buildings provided him some auspicious good fortune: he was awarded the prime site of the three, at the end of the island, with the opportunity for

some of the twenty-nine units to have more than one-hundred-eighty-degree panoramic views.

The apartment buildings create the eastern building wall of Aqua and form the stepping stone down from the higher structures to the east, the generally undistinguished condominiums that line the beach. They also project an image that both pinpoints Aqua's moment in history and simultaneously makes it a seamless part of Miami Beach's historical context, with enough seriousness of architectural purpose and whimsy, deftness of hand (from each of the three architects), and appropriateness of materials to impart a sense of belonging to place. They are at once fresh and familiar.

The architects at DPZ (Fontalvo-Albello was the project manager throughout) laid out the streets and designed the basic townhouse configurations for the forty-six attached houses that would fill out the island. An initial plan called for smaller houses with guest (or "granny") quarters and small courtyard spaces for gardens; marketing studies, however, suggested the houses be larger to meet the demands of a more affluent buyer, and the houses grew by approximately 30 percent. Gone were the courtyards, which became light wells, and the granny flats, which were incorporated into the house. (There are those critics who believe that this was a misstep, that Aqua would have had a better scale and a livelier pedestrian life at a lower price point, but that is Monday-morning quarterbacking of the most improvable sort.) Plater-Zyberk later pointed out that almost everything in the plan was subject to design and redesign, a long process of thinking out the program, but the essential idea for the street spaces never changed. Those streets were to become all-important because they are the very face of urbanism at Aqua, lined with trees and townhouses, carefully measured and paced, creatively placed to maximize the perspectives and views.

At the point that the basic townhouses were being designed, a wish list of architects was set. Because Aqua was set to be a modernist development, Robins and DPZ carefully cultivated their choices. Robins sought some nationally known and even, in one case, edgier architects from New York, including Emanuela Frattini Magnusson and the Iranian-born sisters Gisue and Mojgan Hariri.

Frattini Magnusson, who is the daughter of the famed Italian architect Gianfranco Frattini, was educated in Milan and then worked in London for Charles Fister before coming to New York. She worked in the offices

of the multifaceted designer Tibor Kalman before setting out on her own, establishing a practice—called EFM Design—that embraces architecture, interiors, furniture design, graphics, and more. Frattini Magnusson has designed furniture for Knoll and Montina, among others, and was selected by the American Institute of Graphic Arts as one of four designers to redo its four-story headquarters. In fact, she had collaborated with Gorlin (he did the architecture, while she did the interior design) on a residential renovation in New York. Frattini Magnusson also designed the kitchens (working with Bulthaupt) and the bathrooms throughout Aqua.

The Hariri sisters—whose company is called Hariri & Hariri Architecture—founded their firm in New York in 1986. Both received their architecture degrees from Cornell, Gisue in 1980 and Mojgan in 1981. Mojgan Hariri also received a master's degree from Cornell in 1983. Gisue Hariri worked in New York and San Francisco, while Mojgan apprenticed with the firm of James Stewart Polshek and Partners. Both sisters are known for their theoretical as well as their built work, and for a lively, interactive aesthetic.

In Miami, they had designed a short-lived showroom for the designer Tui Pranich (who in turn bought, decorated, moved into, and sold an apartment in the Chatham building at Aqua). The eight-thousand-square-foot glass-walled showroom had two levels, with concrete floors and a ring of water around its periphery, so that the experience was like that of being on a man-made island. For the Juan Valdez coffee shop in New York's midtown (which was done in collaboration with RIR Architectos in Bogota, Colombia), Hariri & Hariri designed a glass-fronted café; the glass is nestled into a curved teak cocoon that is designed to resemble a coffee bean. Rugged bags of coffee line the window, and an etched stainless steel facade is actually woven metal mesh with a portrait of Juan Valdez applied to it. An otherwise unadorned wall features a continuous slide show of the Colombian coffee industry—farmers, harvesters, and more.

Both Chatham and Gorlin were asked to design townhouses, as well, in both cases a building form well known to them. For other townhouses, Robins and DPZ cast the net across Miami, selecting four architectural firms. Miami native Suzanne Martinson was educated as an interior designer at the University of Florida, then returned to the University of Miami for an undergraduate architecture degree. She then received a master's of architecture from Columbia University and worked, briefly, at Kohn Pederson Fox in New York before returning to Miami to establish her own practice. Allan T. Shulman, a graduate of Cornell University, was an early participant in the University of Miami School of Architecture's Suburb and Town Planning master's program. He too established a solo

practice, but Shulman kept his hand in the academic world as the coauthor (with Jean François Lejeune) of a volume on the Art Deco architect L. Murray Dixon, a scholar of the postwar architect Polevitzky, and the curator of an exhibition on Miami's postwar housing at the Historical Museum of Southern Florida.[14]

Bob Brown and Frank Demandt were once in partnership but now work in independent, though side-by-side, practices. Brown was born in Ohio and grew up in Miami; Demandt, a Canadian by birth, came to Miami by way of Montreal. The two met in college and have architecture degrees from the University of Miami; they came into public attention as young graduates by placing second in a national competition for a bridge over the Miami River. Over the years, their firm became known both for its venturesome abstract work and for buildings that worked well in context.

The final firm chosen to design Aqua's townhouses was Albaisa Musumano. Perhaps the youngest of the group, Aldolfo Albaisa and Thomas Musumano were both graduates of the Rhode Island School of Design and Harvard, and, at the time, teachers at the University of Miami School of Architecture.[15] The two young architects had never seen a project of theirs built, but their theoretical work in regional Modernism had gained them attention.

Plater-Zyberk said that it was clear that the townhouses needed to establish more than a streetscape at Aqua, that there was a larger burden to bear: being an urban prototype that could be adapted regionally, or even with a changed approach to the architecture, in New Urbanist projects elsewhere in the land. Indeed, the whole endeavor was in many ways a prototype for urban infill projects.

In house, DPZ set about creating the templates for the townhouses, in part to achieve the economies of production, so that structural materials and finishes could be ordered in bulk and the builder would not have to deal with an array of forms. The townhouses were basically of a piece, though lots varied in size and typologies changed depending on location. Each street had taller and shorter townhouses, the latter added-in to make space for utilities and telephone lines. Each architect was to design two or three lot types. The process was—especially for DPZ, which is known for assembling all the project architects in a single room for days at a time as they worked together during charrettes—extremely hands off. The designers were asked if they would participate, then given the basic template, dimensions, and certain proscriptions. Thus each of the townhouses had to be at once individual and part of an ensemble.

Brown Demandt's offering is the most classicized, reflecting influences from the Prairie School or Vienna at the turn of the twentieth century. In turn, Frattini Magnusson worked in the tradition of European Modernism, which is her background (she described this as being more in the regional modernist mode: "buildings that express a faith in the future and use elements from the past that make sense"). Her townhouse design at Aqua is in many ways an ode to Le Corbusier, which she said she found apt, particularly in his use of stucco and his affinity for building in warm climates. Martinson, too, made clear reference to Le Corbusier using his "piano balcony," for example. Moving forward, one can see in the designs of DPZ a stripped version of the Modernism of the 1930s and 1940s, houses with definitive proportions that are at once horizontal and vertical (and like Miami Beach's Art Deco buildings express a certain tension between the two forces), and at the same time, tropical with their pale stucco and sheltering eyebrows. Shulman stripped his townhouses even more, as if speaking to the principles found in postwar domestic aesthetic directly, yet his townhouse has a single gable that nods to the nearby Mediterranean residential architecture of Miami Beach.

Both Chatham and Gorlin chose a straightforward modern vocabulary, albeit from a language of the tropics, for their houses, and if one were to carry forward the idea of an architecture that speaks of a century of Modernism, their would represent the ideas and aesthetic of the late twentieth century. Brown later looked back on the process, remarking that the architects had all worked in a vacuum, and noting further that no single design was intended to stand out, saying instead that the value of the townhouses is in the neighborhood they comprise. This neighborhood becomes the residents' domain. It extends beyond the typical curb and fence. It is populated. It extends to the water's edge. The homes' primary social areas reside a few steps above. The second level is of rooms for the family and guests. The third level is a private and commanding master suite. The fourth level is again social, but this time elevated. Upon arrival at this level it is apparent that all of the island homes are penthouses. Their terraces flow into each other, then into the midrise towers of Aqua, and finally into the skyline of Miami Beach beyond.[16]

Once all the designs were submitted, DPZ simply assembled them in a way that made sense, selecting four of one design and three of another, and lining them up along three streets that make up Aqua's low-rise area, using the finished elevations to create the streetscapes. Compositionally, some of the townhouses—particularly Brown Demandt's, DPZ's and Frattini Magnusson's—rely more on a rhythmic relationship of masonry to glass, while others have a higher ratio of glass to stucco. Some rooftops are slightly higher than others, some flat and others less so, to give the streetscape a

Three townhouses by three architects, left to right: Albaisa Musumano, Suzanne Martinson, and Brown Demandt.

kind of skyline. Plater-Zyberk later commented that the whole process was "counterintuitive to the way we work."[17] The firm is usually quite specific at the onset of a project, assigning particular typologies to each location; this was far more random.

Ultimately, each design endured some value engineering from the architect of record Wolfberg Alvarez & Partners; yet if in execution, the townhouses did not fully live up to the full details of the drawings, the full composition compensates. Plater-Zyberk pointed out that urbanism is more forgiving than architecture in that ultimately "the aggregation takes over from the detail."[18] There is also the incremental nature of the design in an urban project. At Aqua, the landscape architecture was begun by

Gary Greenan, a professor at the University of Miami School of Architecture and frequent consultant to the Miami-Dade Planning Department. At the point of execution, the landscape was continued by the consulting firm Kimley-Horn. The landscape is intentionally tropical and even in its infancy was lush; it includes such innovations as a community mango grove, where residents can pluck ripe fruit from the trees. Robins hired the Swiss landscape architect Enzo Enea to design the landscape for his own residence. Enea had not worked in the United States before Robins hired him, first to design a bamboo garden on a sliver of a parking lot in the Design District. The garden is a brilliant study in a layered urban landscape.

At Aqua, the idea was that each homeowner ultimately would have a garden, and that these gardens would not only underscore the tropicality of the landscape but offer differentiations that allow the architecture to become more individual. The streetscape likewise would become more luxuriant with ever-greater tree canopy, ensuring a fully tropical islandlike environment.

Like the landscape, the gatehouse and island-end pool had a progression. Originally, Roberto Behar and Rosario Marquardt, whose work Robins had commissioned in the Design District, were asked to design the gatehouse and pool house. Ultimately, their proposals were supplanted by more straightforward (though nonetheless whimsical) designs from Chatham, who chose to create a kind of underlying narrative for his work, namely that Aqua had been built on a redundant British naval base that had the kind of Moderne architecture one would see in 1930s film set design. His gatehouse and pool house are jaunty and high-spirited, less lofty punctuation marks on a development with some serious aspirations.

Once the townhouses were designed, Robins engaged Proun Space Studio—with principals John Bennett and Gustavo Bonevardi—to develop a four-minute video on Aqua. The firm engages in an array of projects, from houses to museum installations, and as video artists had been part of the team for the "Tribute in Light" at Ground Zero. Part art and part sales pitch, the Aqua video tours the island, offering digital streetscapes and landscapes as well as eerily floating images of the specific buildings, all of which float by to a backdrop of electronic music by William Orbit.

The manifold aspirations of Aqua date back to the very beginnings of the New Urbanism and to the start of DPZ's career. DPZ had already begun confronting some of the attendant issues of more typical suburban pod development in an early project called Charleston Place. There they designed "sideyard houses" in the Charleston prototype but at the same time realized they could not create a real neighborhood behind walls and without a traditional street grid. From there, the ideas flowed, many of them based on DPZ's academic studies of historic towns, beginning with Key West, Florida, but not limited to that; any number of other historic prototypes were brought to bear, including Savannah, Charleston, St. Augustine, Nantucket, and more. In addition, the early studies involved both empirical observation and scientific analysis—the former to judge, for example, how far residents of a neighborhood would walk to school or the bus stop, and the latter to evaluate such planning necessities as curb-cut radii and parking lane dimensions.

The first tenets of New Urbanism were articulated by Duany, Plater-Zyberk, and their several colleagues to include neighborhoods with discernible centers—a town green or central square or an important street corner—and most dwellings built within a short walk, about five minutes, of that center. Some of the urbanistic or architectural characteristics they outlined were intended to promote a kind of spontaneous sociability that had been lost in the sprawl of suburbia. They included a mix of housing types, including "granny flats" in garage apartments, with shops and offices at the edge of the neighborhood and a school and playgrounds within walking distance. Other of the earliest (and still constant) ideas of the New Urbanism were more aesthetic: to work toward a more picturesque environment, drawing residents to the streets, with narrow, tree-shaded sidewalks and buildings set close to frame the space. Another somewhat age-old and forgotten idea was that of terminating street vistas and providing prominent sites for more important, civic buildings.

Under the strictest interpretations, the New Urbanism meets a high set of standards developed over the years articulated in the charter of the Congress for the New Urbanism (CNU), which establishes twenty-seven specific principles to be applied to development. These principles are divided into three categories: first, the region, metropolis, city, town; second, the neighborhood, district, corridor; third, the block, street, and building. Among the more pertinent of these twenty-seven principles are that neighborhoods should be compact, pedestrian-friendly, and mixed-use. Districts generally emphasize a special single use, and should follow the principles of neighborhood design when possible.[19] Other principles discuss a range of activities aimed at encouraging pedestrianism: "Many activities of daily living should occur within walking distance, allowing independence to those who do not drive, especially the elderly and the young. Interconnected networks of streets should be designed to encourage walking, reduce the number and length of automobile trips, and conserve energy."[20]

It was clear from the start that with a mere eight-and-a-half acres and zoning that proscribed mixed uses, Aqua was certainly never going to be

a full-fledged New Urbanist community; further, it became a market reality that in order to attract the high-end buyers Robins sought, the community would have to be gated, a controversial move among New Urbanists. However, DPZ was able to apply many of the important form-based architectural principles to the design of Aqua, so that visually—and in terms of the physical plant—it is indeed New Urbanist. Moreover, it is an apt demonstration of the theories Duany evolved concerning what he terms the "transect": it mediates between two zones, offering a kind of stepping stone from the oceanfront high-rise condominiums to the east as it meets the low-rise single-family neighborhood to the west.

New Urbanism was in its infancy at the start of the design of Seaside in 1983. From there, Duany and Plater-Zyberk, along with Peter Calthorpe, Elizabeth Moule, Stefanos Polyzoides, and Dan Solomon first began to explore the notion that the old, often-unwritten rules of successful urbanism found in urban and suburban neighborhoods and small towns across the country could provide powerful lessons for contemporary designers. As time passed, the number of new projects grew—among them urban infill projects, including some of the United States Department of Housing and Urban Development's Hope Six reconstructions of failed public housing projects—and they became more successful, financially and functionally. Most of the urban projects, however, were low-income interventions or reclaimed brownfields—developments with a higher public purpose— and thus eluded critical scrutiny.[21] This was not so much the case with the discrete projects in more rural and suburban locations in Florida, along the Atlantic coast, and across the country, which became far more synonymous with New Urbanism, if indeed they only represented a portion of what the movement was tackling. These projects include Seaside and the subsequent "towns" along the Florida Panhandle's Route 30A (Rosemary Beach, Watercolor, Alys Beach), as well as Celebration near Orlando, Kentlands in Maryland, I'on Village and the Village at Palmetto Bluff in South Carolina.

One such New Urbanist project, Prospect, detoured from the more common practice of determining an appropriate regional or historic style and then encouraging its use through architectural and other coding. Built on an eighty-acre former tree farm in Longmont, Colorado, Prospect was dubbed "America's Coolest Neighborhood" in the April 2002 issue of *Dwell* magazine. The town was designed by DPZ for developer Kiki Wallace and began with an array of more traditional, Western vernacular architecture, but evolved from there to embrace modernist and even somewhat experimental architecture. As such, Prospect has found a real proponent in Karrie Jacobs, who was *Dwell*'s founding editor and is now an author who writes for *Metropolis* mag-

azine. Though the more modernist houses were not as well received locally as they were on a national level, Jacobs has said that Prospect "features the bravest mix of modern and traditional housing anywhere."[22]

Prospect generated quite a buzz with its step into Modernism, at least in the architectural publishing world, but it wasn't the first New Urbanist town or development to embrace Modernism. That place in history actually would go to Seaside, which many considered to be eighty acres of nostalgic cottages. Seaside's developer, Robert Davis (himself a pivotal figure in the development of the ideas of the New Urbanism), had earlier in his career built a highly experimental modernist townhouse development called Apogee, designed by the Miami architect Bobby Altman, in Miami's Coconut Grove neighborhood. Davis was bred on Modernism, a willing student of his "Auntie Mame," as he called her. A devout modernist in those early, exciting years of the twentieth century, she had lived in Paris as a young Bohemian and bought works by Pablo Picasso and Fernand Leger, which she later sold in favor of geometric expressionists. With her young nephew, she toured museums and galleries, and looked at architecture, honing his taste. At Seaside, Davis would realize that the vernacular architecture he began to build (the earlier houses were far less complex than those built as the town attracted ever-more-affluent residents) "shared some of the qualities of austerity and simplicity" that he had so long admired. He looked for architects who shared this appreciation for austerity and simplicity, as well as a feeling for the sensual, which he pointed out was dominant in the works of Le Corbusier, for example.[23]

In fact, Seaside embraced Modernism early on, with cottages by Walter Chatham (who would go on to become one of Aqua's key designers) and Victoria Casacsco, as well as public buildings by Steven Holl (whose Seaside work was among his earliest built projects), Deborah Bourke, Alexander Gorlin, Rodolfo Machado and Jorge Silvetti, and more. The individual cottages by Chatham and Casasco each received quite a bit of attention. Chatham's was based on the Southern "dog trot" typology but rendered in an experimental modernist fashion and in bright colors—red, turquoise, yellow, blue. *The New York Times* design writer Carol Vogel referred to it as being "at once primitive and sophisticated."[24] With its open, pedimented front and double top-floor porch contained behind multiple louvered shutters, Casasco's house explored several variations on the vernacular. In its July 1990 issue, *Metropolitan Home* called it "a radical twist on small town vernacular" and showed the house on its cover.[25] Chatham's Pugin House bore a relationship to Casasco's, with a two-story gabled and screened porch, the screens held in place by outsized lattice work to reduce the level of articulation. New York's Alexander Gorlin was

an early participant in Seaside and ultimately designed a house for himself (called Stairway to Heaven) that paid full homage to the Bauhaus, and which he considered both an antidote to the more classicized townhouses (some of which he had also designed) along Seaside's Ruskin Place, and an affirmation of the design freedom that the town's code actually allowed.

For Seaside's town center, Davis and DPZ selected a then little-known architect teaching at Columbia University and practicing in New York. Steven Holl had won a PA Award in 1986 for a house on Martha's Vineyard that, though more modern than most of what was then being built at Seaside, seemed to embrace many of the same ideas about adapting the American beach cottage vernacular. For Seaside, Holl built a four-story concrete building that he called the Hybrid Building, as it contained

multiple uses—stores on the ground floor, offices on the second, and apartments on the third and fourth—as well as two quite different facades: a two-story arcade facing the central green and a more idiosyncratic and changing form at the back. Adjoining the Holl building is the Modica Market, designed by Deborah Berke and Carey McWhorter (with DAG Architects of nearby Destin, Florida), again strong and modern with a concrete block and corrugated steel facade, and a two-story arcade bisected by awnings to break down the scale. Berke, ironically enough, was at the time gaining her reputation for the sweet, nostalgic cottages she was designing at Seaside, though also with McWhorter, she designed the more experimental Schmidt House there. Rodolfo Machado and Jorge Silvetti were hired early on (at the time, the firm of Machado & Silvetti had completed only a few buildings, some private houses, and a parking garage at Princeton) to design another of the town center buildings, this one facing the Modica Market and the Hybrid Building.

Early on, too, came Seaside's beach pavilions, which became long-lasting iconic images of Florida tourism; these were shade houses at the peaks of the walkways that took beachgoers over the dunes. The pavilions were each individual works, some more classical and others not. In this latter category came structures designed by such architects as Roger C. Ferri, known for his experimental and theoretical work, who described his Odessa Street Pavilion as "a capriccio on vernacular 'stick' construction … a sand comber's shack … a tropical palm frond hut … a Chippendale fretwork porch that creates shifting kaleidoscopic effects…. It dematerializes from others into a flickering tent of sea and sky."[26] Other pavilions were created by David Coleman of Seattle, who designed a wooden obelisk of fixed louvers; Michael McDonough, who later emerged as a leading experimental voice in architecture, and whose West Ruskin Street Beach Pavilion was a single gable filled in with decorative lattice; and Steve Badanes, also known as the Jersey Devil, who designed a giant umbrella to shade the landing.

The groundwork was set for experimental or modern architecture; the market, however, did not follow. Soon the will of the marketplace became known as the whim of the designers, at least in some academic and critical circles. Yet Duany, in particular, has always persisted in his view that the New Urbanism was not about style.

Aqua's art program was integral to the whole process. Robins assembled a panel of distinguished artists, museum directors, and curators to assess and select the large-scale art that would go into the project. The panel included the California conceptual artist John Baldessari; the New York gallery owner Jack Tilton (who had long been Robins's art advisor); former Whitney Museum director David Ross, a recognized expert on both video art and contemporary art; and Bonnie Clearwater, director of the Museum of Contemporary Art in Miami. Robins was a full participant in the panel. The group met and evaluated a number of well-known artists, some of whom had never worked at a large scale before.

For the two primary public art installations the panel chose Richard Tuttle and Guillermo Kuitca. Tuttle was born in 1941 in New Jersey, educated at Trinity College in Hartford, Connecticut, and subsequently at the Parsons School of Design ASND; he now lives and works in both New York and New Mexico. Tuttle is a sculptor, whose work is generally in three dimensions (though he frequently calls it "painting") and at a small scale—iconoclastic works that critics sometimes term, admiringly enough, bricolage. His work can incorporate an array of mundane and common

RIGHT A panoramic water view from the west.

40

household materials such as bubble wrap, Styrofoam, paper, string, wire, cloth, and other found objects. Initially his work was controversial; Tuttle's first American exhibition at the Whitney provoked the critic Hilton Kramer to proclaim that in some cases "less is less." This unleashed a vast debate (with the primary respondent being Thomas Hess writing in *New York Magazine*) both over Kramer's eye for artists (he had trashed Jackson Pollock and Willem de Kooning in the past) and over Tuttle's work.[27] Tuttle, however, soon gained critical acceptance, to the point that Michael Kimmelman called his most recent Whitney exhibition "a cross between a kindergarten playroom and a medieval treasury" in *The New York Times*, in a review so filled with both information and accolades that it bears quoting at length:

Here are a few things you might not notice in Richard Tuttle's sublime retrospective at the Whitney Museum. Blue gels tint the wall at the entrance that has his early tin "Letters" on it. The lights cast in slight shadow the shallow letters, which are a little like metal versions of toddlers' toys in cryptic alphabet shapes. "Replace the Abstract Picture Plane"—a grid of painted plywood panels, jaunty and framed in white—is off to the right. It looks as if it stands out from the wall. That's because it does, barely: the panels extend beyond their frames by the width of the plywood (or twice that width where the plywood sheets are doubled), while the backs of the picture frames aren't quite flush with the wall. They hang a quarter of an inch away.

Such whispering details, of which there are an endless number here, are at the heart of Mr. Tuttle's rapturous brand of intimism. For 40 years he has murmured the ecstasies of paying close attention to the world's infinitude of tender incidents, making oddball assemblages of prosaic ephemera, which, at first glance, belie their intense deliberation and rather monumental ambition. Never mind the humdrum materials and small scale. In the ambition department, Mr. Tuttle yields no ground to the Richard Serras of this world.[28]

Kuitca, born in Argentina in 1961, began attracting international interest as North American curatorial and collector eyes turned south. His work takes the environment—built and unbuilt, mapped and uncharted—and turns it into abstractions that rely on metaphor and oblique allusion. His paintings often involve the creation of architectural plans that take gridlike form, after which he fills in the spaces in tones of gray, black, brown. The paint begins to obliterate the order underneath. Kimmelman wrote that his work is "cool, airless, philosophical and oblique. It is not surprising that he admires Jorge Luis Borges, his fellow Argentinian. The anonymity of his generic maps, record covers, and architectural plans evokes a psychic space that can rise to a kind of exquisitely hypnotic level. His work is desolate and haunting, and it can be very beautiful when it isn't too arch or glacial."[29]

The critic Ken Johnson said of Kuitca's work, again worth quoting at length,

the overpainting adds a flickering spatial dimension and a weathered appearance, giving the plans an antique look and an aura of historical and possibly magical significance. They might illustrate the visionary writings of Jorge Luis Borges, who Mr. Kuitca has credited as an inspiration.

The relationship between the painterly and the architectural can be read as an interplay between opposed states of mind: between authoritarian order and romantic expression. History and its institutions seem to weigh down the insurgency of the individual, which gives the paintings a dour mood and makes them less playfully inventive than they might be.[30]

Robins asked Susan Richard, a Miami Beach–based artist turned color consultant, to shepherd the works from concept to reality. She recalled that when Tuttle first arrived at Aqua, the entire site was little more than rubble. Eventually the tile mural was conceived for two large walls of the Chatham Building overlooking the adjacent swimming pool. Tuttle and Richard started work with a shallow pan filled with black ink. They then found a stone, tossed it into the pan and let the ink splash onto white paper, thus *Splash* was born. Then, said Richard, it became clear that a maquette was needed, so they turned to the students of the University of Miami. The model they created was then scanned into the computer and

a grid was placed over it; if any speck of black ink fell within a square, that square received a tile. A mathematician was brought into the circle to evaluate the pattern, which he termed "pseudorandom," a term that essentially applies to computer-generated patterns that seem to have no underlying order. The project was then mapped, a process Richard termed "really serious," and the tiles were ordered. The red, yellow, black, and twenty-four-karat-gold tiles came from Turkey, while the white tiles that form the backdrop came from Brazil.

The Kuitca work, entitled *Aquarelle*, involves a pool in what might otherwise have been an unused traffic circle; the pool itself is white terrazzo, with risers that step out of it. The risers could be used as seating or steps, or could simply remain part of the overall visual aspect of the project. Looking down into it, one sees Kuitca's abstracted map version of Aqua, laid out in terrazzo tiles in shades ranging from white to gray. The pool is thirty-one feet long by twenty-six feet wide. The land around it rises up at a steep slope; initially it was grass, but Kuitca bought recycled black rubber turf to surround it, to ensure that it would not be interpreted as a merely decorative fountain.

A third piece of art, by Mark Handforth, was selected from Robins's existing collection. It is a "found object," a telephone pole that was installed, floor to ceiling, in the lobby of the Spear Building, thus imbuing the brand new and pristinely white lobby with a much longer and almost archeological history. Elsewhere in the public spaces of Aqua, representative art from Robins's collection can be seen, including such works as Florian Maier-Aichen's Untitled (*Cloud LAX*) and Mark Grotjahn's Untitled (*Red & White*) in the Gorlin Building lobby. Three works by Jan De Maesschalck can be seen in the Spear Building along with others by Maria Fernanda Cardoso, Jaya Howey, and Amelie von Wulffen. Works by Miami artists Tao Rey and Mette Tommerup are on view in the Chatham Building.

The Tuttle was unveiled during Art Basel 2005; it was not for another year that the Kuitca was completed, and again, launched at an Art Basel party. Though the Kuitca was critically well received, a *New York Times* social reporter, Guy Trebay, did not see it in such flattering terms, writing:

Mr. Kuitca was unveiling *Aquarelle*, a reflecting pool he created at Aqua, Mr. Robins's multimillion dollar residential development, where curb appeal has been ratcheted up with art. Richard Tuttle, for instance, installed a tiled sculpture on two poolside walls there, the tiles meant to represent a splash pattern created by a boulder dropped into the pool. The price tag is reputed to be no drop in the bucket, perhaps as much as $2 million.

Mr. Kuitca's creation is a tiled depression, whose ornamentation looked like a Google Earth view of the Aqua vicinity. As the crab salad tarts were passed in the cool tropical evening and Mr. Robins showed a Shanghai investor around the place, it suddenly came clear that what the Kuitca pool most resembled, set as it was in a moat of shredded rubber mulch the artist found on eBay, was a fancy version of the tub planters one sometimes sees in rural yards.[31]

Aqua has received much attention in the press. Most of it is neither analytical nor thorough. That will come in time. With its condominium ownership, it will pass out of Robins's control and into the hands of the one hundred and fifty-one owners, whose predilections and preferences may change it aesthetically, socially, or organizationally over the course of the years. At Seaside, just to cite one example, the owners chose to replace the more rural shell streets with brick pavements, thereby ridding the town of one of its more rugged-rustic aspects. At Aqua, some controls are in place. Zoning is limited enough that additions would be unlikely, though in an era of building frenzy, almost anything is possible. The City of Miami Beach has a color code, which might mean that radical changes in color would not be allowed. More commerce beyond the single tiny convenience store is unlikely; the gate keeps outside shoppers out, and as of 2007, Aqua was mostly used seasonally, the apartments largely part-time residences. Still, that may change.

The largest age group in the American population, the baby boomers, is at early retirement age now, and if patterns hold, will be shifting its geographic affiliations, moving from places of employment to places of leisure. More jobs are global, often requiring proximity to a major airport rather than to a specific corporate headquarters. Others merely require high-speed computer connections. Further, as needs and populations shift, so does the demand for physicians, therapists, attorneys, and others in the service professions. Miami Beach, which was among the oldest—in terms of chronological age—cities in America in the 1970s, had by the turn of the twenty-first century become one of the youngest, but this demographic is changing again, as middle-aged and early-retirement-aged transplants arrive. Given these demographic and geographic shifts, it seems likely that Aqua will ultimately have more permanent residents. That being said, however, it is also likely that—as a high-end residential enclave in what is essentially a resort city—the composition of residents will not change definitively: it will still have its share of jet-setters, celebrities seeking privacy, and part-timers who use their houses or apartments infrequently.

The gating and exclusivity of Aqua has provoked criticisms from New Urbanists who see the movement as being essentially democratic and aimed at both openness and a kind of equality gained by mixing incomes within the confines of a particular neighborhood. At the Harvard seminar, Krieger asked this question bluntly: "How can you, in your next project, overcome the New Urbanists' criticism of this place by making it less isolated, more mixed-use, and by realizing social diversification." Plater-Zyberk answered with equal bluntness, saying that at Aqua those mandates were for the next generation, to wit, the owners who would take control of Aqua. Plater-Zyberk went on to say that "it's really about remaking places. And this was a remake."[32]

That may seem simple on the surface, but in fact it is a complex idea for much of urban America, be it the densely populated, sophisticated cities of the eastern seaboard and West Coast, or the deteriorating and somewhat abandoned cities that dot the Rust Belt and the Midwest, where corporations have closed and populations have diminished. Appealing urban infill is also of critical importance in the effort to control the kind of leapfrog development that takes place in the countryside and forests outside of more urbanized areas. The implications of this are widespread: from consolidation of city services, to savings of fossil fuel, to curbing the pollutants of gasoline emissions from automobiles stuck in commutes. Viable alternatives have not existed in large enough numbers to bring residents back to the city. Aqua poses one such solution. It is visually appealing and offers some of the spatial enticements of the suburbs—large enough houses, for example.

Plater-Zyberk went on to respond to Krieger this way: "The challenge of remaking is producing a unity of experience out of diversity, whether it is a community of people who want to be socially connected or whether it's a retail where each individual's store depends on the identity of the whole neighborhood or district; it has to do with the same overall vision of all of those efforts, if it is not style. How should old and new fit together in scale and building surface? How can we insert new forms without devaluing beloved existing old ones? New Urbanists are focusing on experiences for the pedestrian, providing frequent enough changes, through doors and windows and a scale for walking rather than driving."[33]

Robins added that the main focus of Aqua was "urban design, enhanced by good architecture and interesting art." The essential key was to be exemplar in so doing, to make Aqua not just another expensive enclave of houses for the very rich, and that indeed called for the best knowledge of urban design, architecture, and art. Perhaps the best metaphor for Aqua can be found in music: it is an orchestral piece—a symphony—rather than a concerto. Each instrument has a moment, some more than others, but in the end it is the full composition that compels.

ABOVE A night shot shows the buildings lighted and etched against the starless sky.

1 The entire list of participants included *Harvard Design Magazine* editor William Saunders, the developer Geoffrey LePlasteir, the builder Bill Tripodl, the architects Alison Spear and Chad Oppenheim, and *The Miami Herald* journalist Andres Viglucci.

2 Krieger, Alex, as quoted in *Harvard Design Magazine*, Spring/Summer 2006, p 135.

3 *Miami Daily News*, July 10, 1924 "Allison Island Nearly Finished."

4 Ibid.

5 Sonji Jacobs, *The Miami Herald,* August 16, 2000 "Historic Hospital Goes to its Reward"

6 DATES of birth and death, the nationally esteemed Alfonso, a Mariel refugee arrived in Miami in 1950–1991 and then in a too-short career ended by AIDS, painted in Los Angeles and Miami.

7 That kind of collaboration was short-lived; after Philippe Starck's redo of the historic Delano Hotel lobby, the city of Miami Beach enacted new preservation laws that governed not just facades but public interiors as well.

8 Interview, 2006.

9 In the same era, Miami's residential modernists worked in a far more American language, influenced more by Frank Lloyd Wright and such Californians as Richard Neutra and Rudolph Schindler.

10 See Stern, Jewel and Jon A. Stuart. *Ely Jacques Kahn, Architect: Beaux-Arts to Modernism in New York* (New York: W. W. Norton & Company, 2006).

11 Interview, 2006.

12 Interview with Ludwig Fontalvo-Abello, 2006.

13 Ibid.

14 *The Florida Home: Modern Living, 1945–1965*, Historical Museum of Southern Florida, June 25, 2004 to January 23, 2005.

15 The firm has since split up.

16 Brown, Bob, interview, 2007.

17 Interview, 2006.

18 Ibid.

19 Charter of the Congress for the New Urbanism.

20 Ibid.

21 DPZ's involvement in the reconstruction of New Orleans is an exception to this in that it was been highly publicized.

22 Jacobs, Karrie, I am the Uncool Hunter, *Metropolis*, May 2004.

23 Interview, 2007.

24 Vogel, Carol, Design: Double Standards, *The New York Times Magazine*, April 30, 1989.

25 *Metropolitan Home,* July 1990.

26 Roger Ferri quoted in Mohney, David and Keller Easterling, *Seaside: Making a Town in America*, Princeton Architectural Press, 1991, p. 208.

27 Kimmelman Michael, *40 Years of Making Much out of Little*, November, 11 2005.

28 Op. cit.

29 Kimmelman, Michael, *Art inReview*; Guillermo Kuitca, November 22, 2002.

30 Johnson, Ken Guillermo Kuitca, "Castle to Castle," *The New York Times*, May 21, 1999.

31 Trebay, Guy, "Miami Basel: An Art Costco for Billionaires," *The New York Times*, Dec. 4, 2006.

32 *Harvard Design Review*, op. cit.

33 *Harvard Design Review*, op. cit.

LIVING AT AQUA

GATEHOUSE

THE FACT OF THE GATEHOUSE and the actual Aqua gatehouse are two separate issues here. The architect, Walter Chatham, acknowledges that many observers "can't get past the idea that there is a gate." And indeed, the New Urbanism generally proscribes walled-off or gated and guarded communities, but at Aqua, it was an economic reality that the high-end buyers of the apartments and townhouses wanted that extra perceptual layer of security.

To design the gatehouse, Chatham conceived a narrative of Aqua as a former naval base or waterside industrial facility with a sentry post at the entrance, thus a kind of ship-inspired aquatic design. Appropriately, that same nautical impulse provided fodder not only for Miami Beach's Art Deco architecture but later for its postwar modern buildings, as well as the Googie icons more dominant in Los Angeles but also found in South Florida.

The gate is at the pedestrian level but is also architecturally overscaled and simplified. It not only grounds Aqua but sets the mood, preparing the visitor for an uplifting architectural experience.

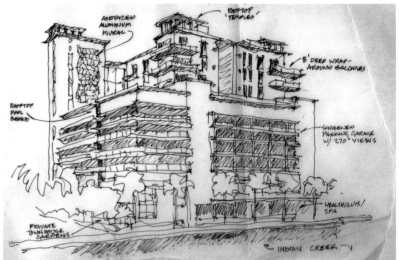

THIS PAGE AND
FACING PAGE Three
views of the Chatham building, from the street, as a
sketch, and from the water.

CHATHAM BUILDING

WALTER CHATHAM was given the only building remaining from the St. Francis Hospital Complex to retrofit and transform into Aqua's parking garage with sixteen units above. Chatham had, in the past, renovated large-scale commercial structures and designed single-family houses, but he had never before put the two together. In this project, however, he confronted what he aptly called "the ugliest building in Miami Beach," with its Chattahoochee-stone cladding. The generally dirty-looking and unpleasant structure was, like so many buildings of its late-1960s era, a product of the kind of one-dimensional modernist thinking that with a solution to the functional problems, a form will follow.

Yet as Chatham peered beneath the off-putting stone aggregate cladding, he discovered that the building's massing was actually quite

LEFT The exercise room at Chatham Building.

RIGHT A terrace at the Chatham Building.

pleasing. He reclad the structure in two shades of pale blue-gray stucco panels, with metal louvered sunscreens suspended over the garage facade, then adapted the rooftop residential area—which had been the St. Francis Hospital psychiatric ward—to accommodate apartments. He felt that the original building looked like the base of a much taller building with a top "that someone had taken a chainsaw and knocked off." To improve that truncated silhouette, he added towers at the ends of the roofline, giving the building a far more urban and engaging silhouette.

To offset the repetitive mass of the garage, Chatham added a series of whimsical, decorative parallelograms in aqua, blue, and yellow. The ground-floor lobby, a stopping off point for many visitors to Aqua who park in the garage, was added to the existing building with the purpose of creating what Chatham called a "floaty, planar" roof over a bright, sun-infused space with floor-to-ceiling glass walls and an oval skylight to let visitors feel as if they were outside. Pale chartreuse doors lead into the lobby, where one wall is painted a bright pumpkin hue, others are clad in marble, and the floors are gray-green tile. The concierge desk is also marble-topped. The lobby's iconic chrome, leather, and glass modern

PRECEDING PAGES
Lap pool at Chatham Building.

RIGHT
The Children's Learning Center/playroom at the Chatham Building, with wall and ceiling paintings by Beatrice Rich.

LEFT
Chatham Building lobby.

furniture was selected in conjunction with Luminaire's Jennifer Sang and the interior designer Simona Ciancetta.

Chatham sought to have the residential spaces of the building evoke the idea of the grand apartments and ocean liners of the 1930s: big, airy spaces with high ceilings and tall windows. An industrial-inspired decorative bracket supports the balconies, adding interest to the rooftop design. The penthouses have roof gardens, and the towers, though designed to give the building a more felicitous way to meet the sky, serve a functional purpose with outdoor kitchens, baths, and showers.

PETER AND KATHERINE
GREENSPUN APARTMENT

ABOVE Living room and view toward balcony of Peter and Katherine Greenspun Apartment in the Chatham Building.

RIGHT Dining room and kitchen.

FOLLOWING PAGES
A north-facing balcony view for the Peter and Katherine Greenspun Apartment in the Chatham Building.

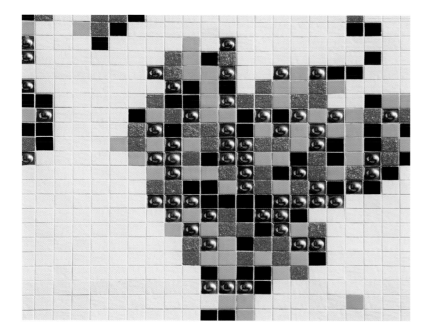

RICHARD TUTTLE, *SPLASH*

The artist Richard Tuttle, long known and much praised for his small-scale work, had never before done a project that was either large or architectural. Working with the Miami-based consultant Susan Richard, Tuttle conceived a vast tile mural that would work both as a building wall and an aesthetic statement to be seen by Aqua residents and passing boaters alike. The south-facing tile mural covers a wall of the Chatham Building alongside Aqua's lap pool.

Tuttle did the drawings for *Splash* on site in an unusual process. He and Richard filled a shallow pan with black ink and then took a stone and tossed it in to see how the ink would land on a sheet of paper held vertically alongside the ink pan. From there, the two hired University of Miami art students to create a model, and from both the drawing and the model began the hard work of mapping the mural.

The wall of the model was scanned into the computer, and a grid was placed over it. If the ink marks fell into a square of the grid, that square would get a tile. A mathematician was found to calculate the pattern, which he determined was "pseudo-random," a numerical sequence that can be generated with algorithms. The mural was then mapped and turned into a template that was, in sequence, turned into tile. The tile itself came from Turkey, with twenty-four-karat gold tiles providing the sun-glinted highlights for *Splash*.

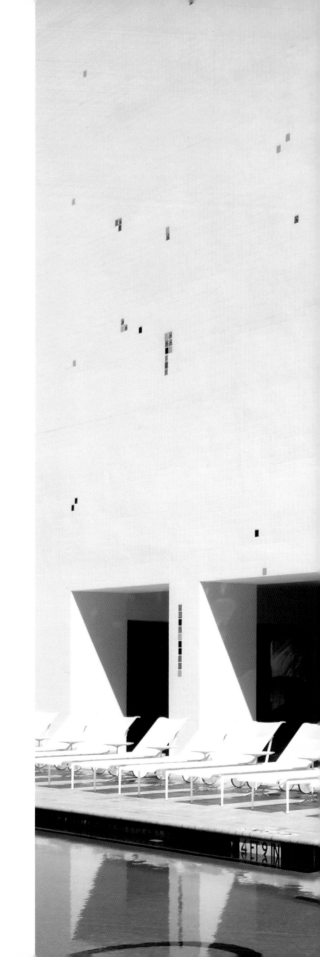

SPEAR BUILDING

AS A NATIVE MIAMIAN, the architect Alison Spear wanted to design a building that was at once personal and universal. Like developer Craig Robins, she too was born on the Aqua site at St. Francis Hospital, which made the job of designing the first of two midrise apartment buildings even more significant. Spear invoked early memories of modernist Miami buildings to take a controversial step and create a vertical row of apartments with enclosed balconies that are essentially glassed-in porch spaces. (Conventional market savvy might have suggested that those would be hard to sell, but in fact, the units with all-glass "outdoor rooms" were the first to be bought.) From the outside, these enclosed spaces read as glass cubes, adding interest to the composition.

The building does indeed pay homage to Miami postwar modern architecture, both in terms of its clean lines and its slightly abstracted architectural allusions. At the top is an oval smokestack, a reference both to the streamlined ship design of earlier eras and to Morris Lapidus's Eden

Roc Hotel. Likewise, Spear used tile, a favored material in the early years after World War II, but her tile is added to the building impressionistically. She took close-up photographs of the surging surf of the Atlantic Ocean and transformed those images into a pixilated pattern, which was then iterated in an applied mosaic in sun-glinted blues, aquas, and golds that seem indeed like a frothing wave in the sea. The building itself is white, with clear glass balcony rails and tinted blue glass windows at the lower levels. Aqua's small convenience store is in one corner of the building.

For Spear, the interiors assumed equal importance to the exterior design, both in terms of the public lobby spaces and the apartments. Her lobby features one of Aqua's three large-scale works of art, in this case a "telephone pole" by the Miami artist and scholar Mark Handforth. The lobby furniture, designed by Spear and made by Odegard in India, is a wood substructure wrapped in silvery metal with blue and green upholstery that reiterates the sea-blue-greens of the tile pattern on the facade. The walls and floors are clad in a polished terrazzo, white on white, and Spear also designed hand-knotted wool carpets that were manufactured in India by Odegard. The apartments themselves were left as open as possible, with the idea that they would be grand spaces with as few walls as possible, to be inviting and to express the idea of what it means to live in the tropics.

MARK HANDFORTH, *FREEBIRD*

THE MIAMI ARTIST MARK HANDFORTH works with found objects, some of them at a large scale. This indeed is the case with *Freebird*, which is a telephone pole formerly used by the electric company, Florida Power and Light. The piece was already in Aqua developer Craig Robins's art collection rather than commissioned specifically for his island development like the two artworks by Richard Tuttle and Guillermo Kuitca. Yet it seemed entirely appropriate and thus was placed in the lobby of architect Alison Spear's midrise building, the Spear Building.

Handforth noted that the pole, made of Western cypress, had absorbed decades of history and endured climate, change, growth, and more. "The nicks and chips are the hidden story," he said. As an artist, he is intrigued with such metaphorical ideas as the transplanting of an object that has borne witness to so much into an environment that is brand new and thus has witnessed little. The act of doing so changes the role of the light pole and further changes the building lobby into which it was placed, giving each of them an additional layer of meaning.

THIS PAGE Mark Handforth's *Freebird* is part of the Spear Building lobby, which features furniture designed by Alison Spear.

HAL TAYLORSON
APARTMENT

RIGHT The Hal Taylorson Apartment in the Spear Building looks out at Indian Creek and features a one-thousand-square-foot lanai.

TOP Living room with painting by
Jordan Eagles entitled *Ultimate Rebirth*.

ABOVE Master bedroom.

RIGHT Kitchen.

FOLLOWING PAGES
View looking east.

AURELIO AND PEPIS LOPEZ ROCHA APARTMENT

RIGHT The Rocha Apartment in the Spear Building, interior design by Crea, Simona Ciancetta, includes furniture by Phillipe Starck, Karim Rashid, and Piero Lissoni, among others.

MARK MUTCHNIK
APARTMENT

RIGHT Mark Mutchnik's residence in the Spear Building was designed and built by Mutchnik Construction Group Inc.

The master bedroom features a custom wall unit, wood floor, and a custom-made bed.

LEFT AND FACING PAGE Two views of the kitchen.

FOLLOWING PAGES The living room, which features custom cabinetry and Venetian stucco walls.

APARTMENT DESIGNED BY
EMANUELA FRATINI MAGNUSSON

ABOVE AND RIGHT
Detail of balcony and balcony view.

FOLLOWING PAGES
Living room of apartment designed by Emanuela Fratini Magnusson in the Spear Building.

GUILLERMO KUITCA, *AQUARELLE*

THE ARGENTINE ARTIST GUILLERMO KUITCA'S site-specific sculpture *Aquarelle* sits in the middle of what might otherwise have been an ordinary traffic island midway between Aqua's Chatham and Spear buildings. The shallow, oval pool is fifteen feet long by nine feet wide, and though it is actually excavated six feet into the ground, wide terrazzo steps lead down to the water, making the pool an experience more than a deep-water basin.

On the floor of the pool, Kuitca created an impressionistic map of Aqua, showing the outlines of the eight-and-a-half acres on which the development was built. The terrazzo in the work ranges from pure white to gray. Kuitca collaborated with the Italian firm Fantini Mosaici to produce the tiles.

The idea behind the work is that it is an oversized and overly idealized painting executed in three dimensions. The layer of water over the already obscured map of the island distorts it further, making the geography essentially unrecognizable.

The fountain is intended as a communal gathering space, where residents of Aqua can gather along the edges or step down into the water. Surrounding *Aquarelle*, and giving it a more surreal quality, is turf of recycled black rubber cut into small pieces as if it were artificial mulch.

TOP
A detail of *Aquarelle*.

ABOVE AND RIGHT
Two views of the artist's pool.

GORLIN BUILDING

SEEN FROM ABOVE, the tip of Allison Island takes the shape of the
prow of a ship, and Alexander Gorlin's apartment building reinforces
that. Gorlin felt full appreciation for the prominent site he was given. The
building itself is wedge-shaped, a study in both sculpture and geometry with flat walls that shift at slight angles as they make their way along
the water's edge. Gorlin thought of it as an exploration of planes and
space, and at the same time a study in shadows and light. Its geometry
also denotes the four cardinal points of the compass, another oblique
navigational reference.

One overarching idea for the building was that it should be as respon-
sive as possible to the sometimes-harsh weather conditions of the tropics:
the searing sun, fierce summer rains, and high humidity. Thus Gorlin
designed deep balconies with additional metal louvers that act as sun-
shades to the residential unit below. The penthouses are set back from the
lower floors and topped with a swooping airfoil (intriguingly both contemporary and an allusion to the postwar period of infatuation with air
travel) in an effort to give the eight-story midrise tower a base, a middle,
and a top.

TOP, BELOW AND FACING PAGE Views of the facade of the Gorlin Building by Alexander Gorlin.

FOLLOWING PAGES The Gorlin Building lobby features a drawing by Mark Grotjahn and a painting by Albert Oehlen.

Out front, there is a triangular-shaped port cochère supported on lozenge columns with three circular openings punched through the canopy, a reference to the Miami Beach architect Morris Lapidus, who used what he called "cheese holes" as one of the trademarks of his design. Inside, the public spaces have polished terrazzo floors and walls that are painted in pastel shades: aqua, pale lavender, light mint green. At one end of the building is a party room with a bar and an exquisite view south along the Indian Creek Canal. A fractured mirror on the opposite wall extends the space, Gorlin said, "in the Cubist manner," an inverted zigzag in three sections. The room also has, in homage to Lapidus's staircases to nowhere, a set of steps to the second floor that can be used for grand entrances of sorts, though it actually does go somewhere, to a second-floor meeting room. Silver lamé curtains from Knoll help dramatize the room, reflecting and refracting the light.

Gorlin designed the small, double-height lobby to offer a sense of arrival. The lobby has a feature wall for art, and Gorlin chose a bright red sculptural sofa by Edra for the space. He said his goal was to have a minimal number of items with maximal effect. The concierge desk lights up to add to the theatrical effect of the lobby.

Gorlin's own Aqua apartment is in this eponymous building, a unit with a dramatic and fairly panoramic view to the south, east, and west (pages 116–121). He thus treated it as a continuation of the water. The floors are

clad in pale stone, and the walls are a light blue-gray. He furnished it with a number of artist-designed and singular furniture pieces—including a textured rug and a stone bench—with the idea that he would anchor the space at the center. There is a glass table from Afra and Tobia Scarpa and a Gaetano Pesce vase, as well as a painting by Sean Mellyn entitled *Girl Named Brancusi* to help complete the room. "Because it was a vacation apartment for myself," he said, "I chose the most beautiful objects I could. I wanted it to impart the ideas of fun and beauty—and relaxation."

ALEXANDER GORLIN
APARTMENT

THIS PAGE Alexander Gorlin's apartment in the building he designed features both collectable furniture, by such designers as Marc Newsom, Ingo Maurer, Isamu Noguchi, and Constantine Grcic, and an art collection that includes paintings by Maja Korner (above) and Byron Kim (right) and a photograph by Tracy Rose (also right).

LEFT AND RIGHT Two views of the living room show a Marc Newsom chair (above and right) and a painting entitled *A Girl Named Brancusi* by Sean Mellyn (right, and also seen on pages 114–115).

FOLLOWING PAGES Another view of the living room, which shows the undulating "column" by Judith Niedermaier and the coffee table that seems to be river stones but is actually synthetic, designed by Andrea Salvetti.

DAVID PARKER AND
MARIAN DAVIS APARTMENT

RIGHT The balcony of
the David Parker and Marian
Davis Apartment in the
Gorlin Building.

ABOVE Kitchen.
RIGHT The living room features paintings by Lynne Gelfman with furniture from Luminaire.

Apartment interior design by Rene Gonzalez.

RIGHT The bedroom with its corner windows.

FOLLOWING PAGES Another view of the living room, offering a magnificent panorama of the distant city skyline.

LEVITAS-WILSTERMAN
RESIDENCE

RIGHT View from
the balcony of the Levitas-
Wilsterman apartment in
the Gorlin Building.

FOLLOWING PAGES
The living room features
a collage by Mimi Levitas.

ABOVE A reading area in the apartment.

RIGHT The dining room features a 1930s-era Murano glass chandelier. Koi chairs surround the table.

ARI WAY

DUANY PLATER-ZYBERK & COMPANY TOWNHOUSE

THE DUANY PLATER-ZYBERK & COMPANY townhouses are in many ways the parent of the other townhouse designs (there are thirteen different designs in all, with nine architects' hands at work) in that the dimensions and layouts formed the baseline for the rest of the development. The DPZ townhouses are at once modern and referential, with a clear allusion to the historic fabric of Miami Beach and its late moderne and early modern stucco buildings.

DPZ is responsible for six of the townhouses, all of them corner units, but three have the narrower twenty-four-foot width, and three are thirty feet wide. These particular townhouses are clustered at the northern and

more urban end of Aqua, near the arterial street that divides the denser New Urbanist development from the historic single-family enclave that occupies the other portion of Allison Island.

The townhouse designs were drawn from the great models of both European and American urbanism. The architect recalls Miami Beach's earlier architecture with classical proportions, symmetry, and a minimum of ornament. Concrete eyebrows over the windows provide shade within, and windows allow for flow-through ventilation, courtyards, and terraces. The interiors have an open plan that is in turn subdivided into traditional rooms to create elegant living spaces. At the fourth level, a tower and rooftop terrace offers long views across the island, letting the occupant look over the buildings of Aqua and out onto the water beyond.

LEFT, RIGHT AND FACING PAGE Views of the facade of the Duany Plater-Zyberk & Company townhouse.

Interiors in a Duany Plater-
Zyberk & Company town-
house; interiors are designed
by Crea, Simona Ciancetta.
The living room (pages
144–145) showcases paint-
ings by Martin Oppel and
Ebehard Havekost.

BROWN AND DEMANDT TOWNHOUSE

THE TOWNHOUSES designed by the firm of Brown Demandt have a cosmopolitan and dignified aesthetic of early European Modernism. The buildings seem as if they could be found in Vienna, Berlin, or Paris, or even Chicago. The design is more articulated than most of the other townhouses at Aqua: elegant and restrained, and yet definitively modern. The architect, Bob Brown, had over the years been interested in a range of architectural history that spanned the late nineteenth and early twentieth centuries but said that here he was striving to create "a punctuation mark" that would be compatible with much of the work he knew from Duany Plater-Zyberk & Company.

Given that, Brown Demandt sought a design that would be part of a greater whole, that would express the idea of life in a "cohesive, secure neighborhood" and also impart a sense of sheer urbanity. The firm designed four grander-scaled end units and five midblock houses. The design is both dignified and playful, as a reworking of the Miami Beach modernist vernacular with "the rendering of a thoughtful countenance" as a primary compositional goal.

The enclosed portions of the house diminish in size on the upper floors, allowing for capacious yet sheltered outdoor terraces. Brown Demandt conceived of the interior spaces as "a village within the village," with the idea that the design would be repeated, rather than being the "one-off" architecture that applies to many single-family houses.

156

ABOVE AND RIGHT
Front view of townhouses
designed by Brown
Demandt Architects.

FOLLOWING PAGES
Perspective view of
townhouse.

AQUA PATH

ZOE WAY

LAGUNA PATH SOUTH AND LAGUNA DRIVE WEST

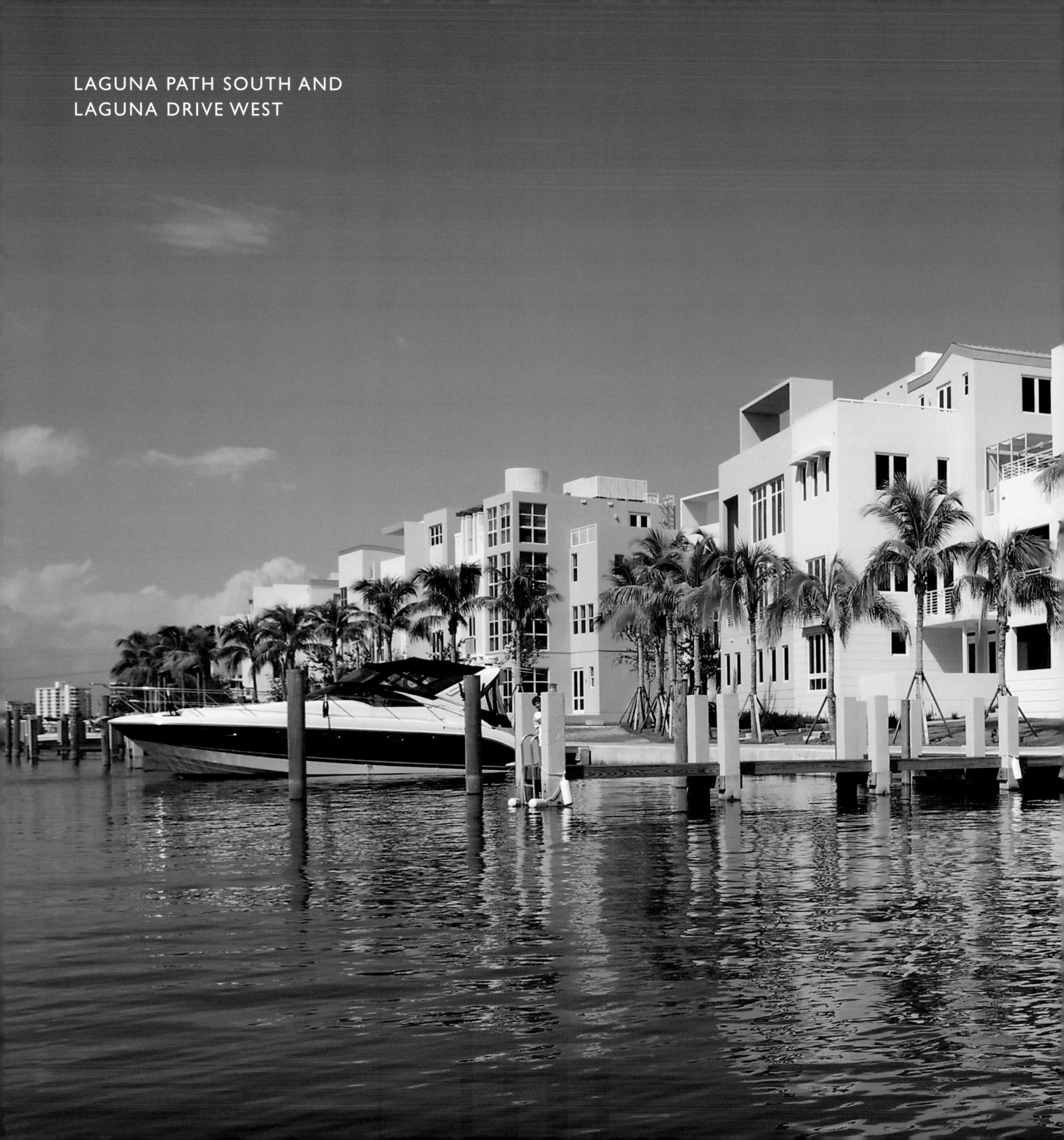

HARIRI & HARIRI TOWNHOUSE

THE SISTERS GISUE AND MOJGAN HARIRI took inspiration for their Aqua townhouse from the facts of its place: that Allison Island was indeed an island, with the waters of Indian Creek surrounding it and boats passing by. They also took cues from their study of Miami Beach today, from the fact that, as Gisue Hariri said, it is "really an overlap of cultures" that range from Cuban to European and more. They found Miami to be sensuous, sexy, and essentially free, and in their design, they sought to bring all of these varying impulses together—location, culture, atmosphere— and create a design that "captured the spirit of Miami."

In general, the Hariri sisters work with specificity, seeking to create designs that meet the very needs and personality of a particular client. In this case, Aqua was speculative housing and so no client existed, per se. Thus, their impulse to design houses that are an extension of a personality had to be channeled into a more generalized idea of the eventual occupants of their three dramatic townhouses.

LEFT A sketch of the Hariri & Hariri Townhouse.

FACING PAGE AND FOLLOWING PAGES Corner and side views of the townhouse.

The roofs arc upward as if to take a scoop out of the sky, an inspiration drawn from the passing boat traffic. The houses are sculptural and yet in a way ephemeral, as the rooflines curve in varying directions and the sun reflects at ever-changing angles. For Hariri & Hariri, the townhouse typology poses a "complex and interesting problem," one in which the narrowness of the building dictates the form, and in which there are usually no more than two facades. The Hariri & Hariri house, however, was an end-of-the-block unit, which gave the architects three elevations.

A primary idea was to break up the volume, as if a single solid block had been carved away. Another innovation was to place three bedrooms at the ground level and raise the living spaces to the second floor as well as the fourth floor, where rooftop terraces connect with a studio suite. There is a courtyard at the entryway, and the second-floor living area also has a large terrace.

SUZANNE MARTINSON ARCHITECTS
TOWNHOUSE

SUZANNE MARTINSON has two different townhouses at Aqua: the largest and one of the smallest. Her large corner house features a two-story balcony that starts on the second floor and rises to the fourth, providing an expansive view of the water beyond. This outdoor room mirrors exactly the living room inside, with the same volumetric space. Martinson wanted to probe the idea of tropical living within modernist spaces with an open plan and thus kept the detailing minimal and the rooms as open as possible.

LEFT Dining area.

FACING PAGE Intimate balcony with water view.

The two-story loggia gives the house a kind of outsized grandeur, making a powerful statement; it is the house's major architectural gesture. The doors between the living room and the loggia can be flung wide open to allow for a true indoor-outdoor space. There are four of these houses, each sitting on a corner site along the water's edge, overlooking the docks in Indian Creek. Martinson's other townhouse design is for a midblock location and is far more straightforward, with wide ribbon bands of windows and a piano balcony (there are three of this typology).

For both the large and small houses, she relied on nautical references such as portholes, exterior stairways with pipe railings, and flag posts, all of which also provide geographic reference to Miami Beach's Art Deco architecture. Martinson drew ideas from Le Corbusier, including the piano balcony. Wherever possible, she added natural light, through large windows and skylights.

**FACING PAGE,
ABOVE AND RIGHT**
Various views of Suzanne
Martinson Architects
townhouse.

ADOLFO ZAYAS-BAYAN ALBAISA AND KRISTOPHER MUSUMANO TOWNHOUSE

FOR THE FIRM of Albaisa and Musumano, working in Aqua was a first. Prior to this townhouse, the two had been teachers and had completed work only in the theoretical realm. The idea behind the townhouse was to be both timeless and, in the same framework, specific—to speak to the architectural traditions of Miami Beach and yet reflect the contrast and complexity that are particular to the tropical climate.

The house has a sculptural quality and an asymmetrical aesthetic. A sheltering concrete arm seems to envelop the fourth-floor rooftop space, and an oversized concrete three-sided frame turns the glass at the second level into a true "picture window." The entrance to the house, likewise, is set off to one side, a vertical concrete louvered screen rising above it.

The architects' focus was on creating a tropical house that would encourage outdoor living. Said Musumano, "We were interested in the idea of extending domestic rituals into the outside space." Thus, at the center of the house is an atrium, and as the building rises, there are also terraces and balconies of varying sizes, shapes, and scale, some more public and others private. These outdoor spaces also provide light and free-flowing ventilation.

WALTER CHATHAM
ARCHITECTS TOWNHOUSE

FOR HIS TOWNHOUSE DESIGN, Walter Chatham sought to maximize the views, not just the long view to the water but also the internal street view, which he felt brought its own intrinsic beauty to Aqua. He chose not to change the layout offered as a beginning point by Duany Plater-Zyberk & Company, as he found the interior design to be most compatible with his ideas for the house.

THIS PAGE
Two views of roof terrace and beyond.

FOLLOWING PAGES
Living room (200–201).

A guesthouse bedroom in the Chatham townhouse (202–203).

Chatham instead went for "maximum glass," with the idea that the design of his townhouse—there are three of them within Aqua—be simple enough to provide a calming influence on both the house's occupants and passersby. The original design called for the addition of large-scaled Bahama shutters, but those were not included in the eventual build-out.

His design relies on "articulated volumes" with a smooth stucco finish and crisp detailing. The townhouses have roof terraces with pipe railings. Chatham designed these to evoke the feeling of being on a ship—a possibility on a small island—and to capture the essence of Miami Beach's historic architecture.

EMANUELA FRATTINI MAGNUSSON
TOWNHOUSE

"THE WORK THAT I DO comes from my education, my background, and the European modernist tradition," said Emanuela Frattini Magnusson of her townhouse design. For her, Modernism is not a style necessarily but more of an architectural credo that expresses faith in the future and uses elements from the past as they make sense. Hers is a regional Modernism.

For her townhouse design at Aqua, she drew definitively from the ideas of Le Corbusier, with the realization that there was "a real affinity" between his works and the architecture that would be appropriate to Miami Beach; this, she pointed out, can be seen in Le Corbusier's use of stucco and his preference for building in warm climates, particularly along the Mediterranean. She also—at least for the colors used in her houses—turned to such sources as the Casa Malaparte in Capri.

Frattini Magnusson's Aqua townhouse was designed with a strong emphasis on both compositional elements and fenestration, using window openings in particular to create shadow lines. With an eye to climate, Frattini Magnusson used overhangs and covered outdoor spaces, as well as cross-ventilation, letting the functional aspects of working in Miami Beach's subtropical climate create the more formal aspects of the design. She purposely chose not to use any formal applied ornament in the design but rather let the corner windows and staircase windows work as decoration.

Frattini Magnusson also designed the European-influenced kitchens and bathrooms throughout Aqua.

AQUA TERRACE

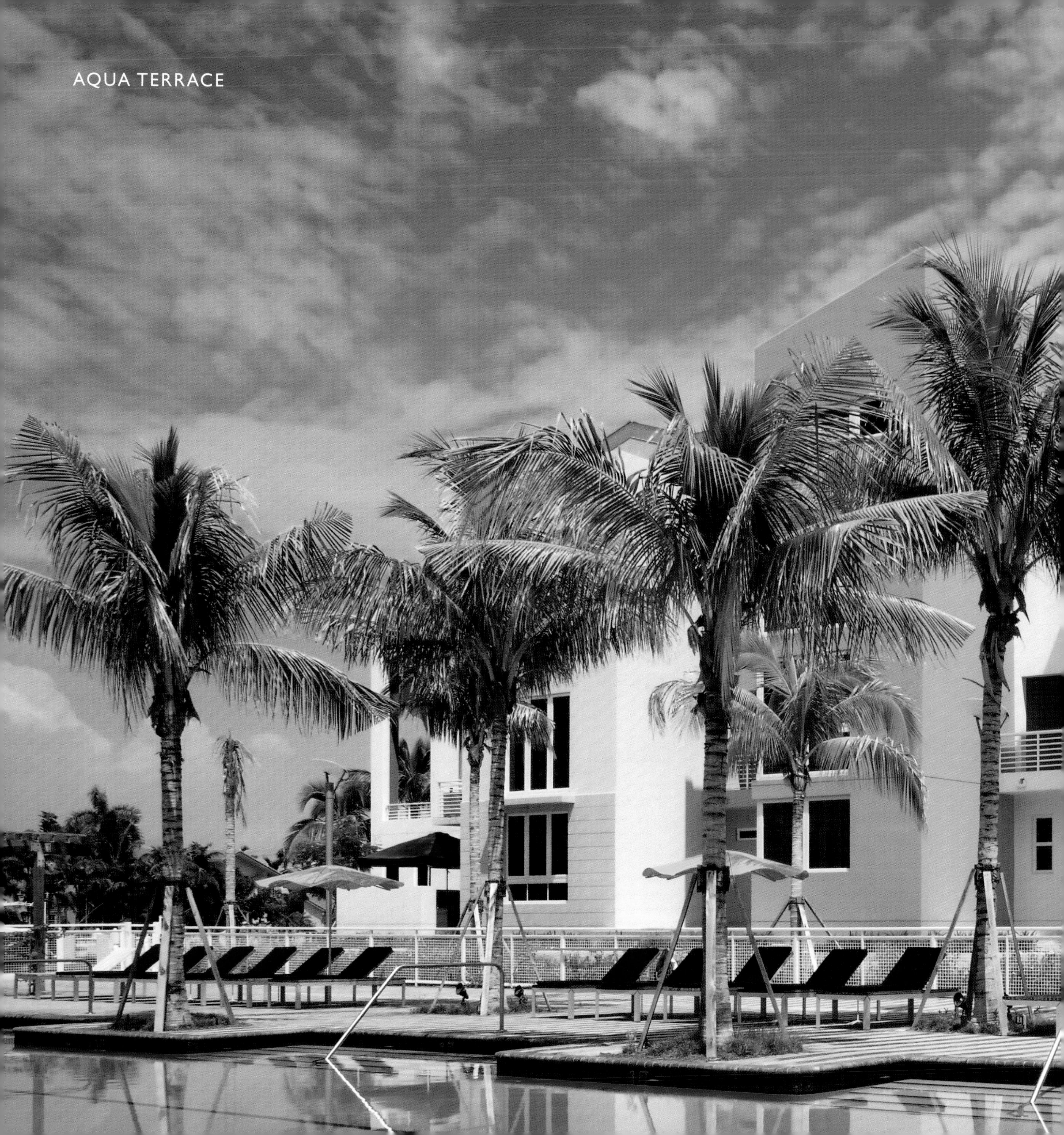

ALLAN SHULMAN ARCHITECTS TOWNHOUSE

FOR ALLAN SHULMAN, the primary goal of the design was to create a series of changing outdoor spaces, so that each of the townhouse's four floors would connect to the outdoors. At ground level, there is a central patio that is enclosed on all four sides. The second floor has a covered porch, while on the third floor, there is a patio marked by a trellis and a canvas canopy. The fourth floor features an open-air roof deck. The outdoor spaces are not stacked but rather spiral up and around the house.

Shulman sought to work in an architectural style that would not only relate to the New Urbanism but would also capture the ideas of Miami Beach's his-

toric building traditions. Thus, his design is at once modern and referential, with a gabled roof at the top that nods to some of the city's earliest buildings and makes reference to the Mediterranean houses in the single-family residential neighborhood to the west of Aqua, while not ignoring Miami Beach's tradition of postwar Modernism.

Each of his four townhouses has a partial corner exposure but, as the designs line up, Shulman's own is always one away from the corner. By experimenting with the four different outdoor spaces, Shulman found that he could bring a clear volumetric organization to the house.

CRAIG ROBINS RESIDENCE

**RIGHT AND FOLLOW-
ING PAGES** The Craig
Robins Residence (pages
216–220) in a townhouse by
Allan Shulman features furniture
by Gio Ponti and Thomas
Dixon. The paintings are
by Ebehard Havekost, John
Baldessari, and Thomas Scheibitz
as well as a sculpture by Paul
McCarthy. An avid collector of
art and design, Robins has employed the assistance of design
curator Ambra Medda and the
gallerist and designer Amy Lau.

CLEMENT G

ESTHETIC JUDG
IN THE IMMEDIAT
THEY COINCIDE
AFTERWARDS TH
ESTHETIC JUDG
YOU CAN NO
TO LIKE A WOR
TO HAVE SUGAR
(WHETHER OR
HONESTLY REP

RIGHT
Bedroom in the Craig Robins
Residence.

ALEXANDER GORLIN ARCHITECTS TOWNHOUSE

ALEXANDER GORLIN'S TOWNHOUSE is purposefully simple. Gorlin, who designed the eponymous Gorlin Building at Aqua's southeastern tip, sought a design that would provide, as he put it, "a moment of relief." Thus, the architecture is as uncomplicated as possible. He thought of it as a kind of "vertical punctuation mark."

Gorlin's townhouse is a narrow midblock type. The roof rises at a slant to a peak at the corner. The building's front facade steps back along the street to give the idea of an extremely slim building. This also allowed the architect to create a second, albeit lower, tower along the urban street wall, as well as an indented entryway. Gorlin attached a romantic background to the design idea, evoking the vernacular houses of Italian hill towns and the works of the fourteenth-century painter Giotto. His idea was to interpret and abstract this in a contemporary version of an Italian tower, as if a house in San Gimignano had been shipped across the Atlantic and recast in modern stucco.

The house form, which is repeated three times, is organized around a courtyard in the center, again relying on the proportions of a small Italian house. The living room is on the second floor and looks out onto the street with a large window. The bedrooms are on the top floor.

WALTER CHATHAM POOL
AND POOL HOUSE

THE FAMILY SWIMMING POOL at Aqua sits at the very tip of the island, a bold move on the part of the developer and the designers, as that is the project's prime real estate. Still, with the idea that this would be a New Urbanist development, Aqua was designed to encourage sociability and to encourage pedestrian activity. One must walk to the swimming pool.

Walter Chatham was selected to design the pool and pool house. He created a rectilinear pool with shallow steps leading into the water. He had practical and philosophical reasons for so doing, first that he wanted it to be easy to get in and out of the pool, and second that he wanted the space to be easy, relaxed, and convivial. Palm trees step down to the water's edge.

With its funnels and bright-colored porthole windows, the little pool house is jaunty and naval-inspired. Chatham designed it not only to make reference to Miami Beach's Art Deco architecture but also to evoke a 1930s British Moderne naval installation; he was inspired by the set design of the BBC films of Agatha Christie's Hercule Poirot. The high spirits of the design are reinforced by the striped paving surrounding the pool.

224

AQUA PROJECT CREDITS

DACRA

Craig Robins
Steven Gretenstein
David Holtzman
Jack Tufano
Ross Baron
Eric Nesse
Elizabeth Guyton
Mary Gomez
Anna Williams
William Tripodi
Cesar Romero
Jacqueline Albuerne
Mayda Horstmann

AQUA REALTY

Stacy Robins
Harvey Daniels
Hank Berg
Kenneth Schwartz
Carolina Oliva
Katie Lillis
Chris Sisino
Jennifer Hernandez

BRIDGEHOUSE

Amy Turkel
Cristine Pacheco
Nikole Augsten
Jennifer Wallace

WOLFBERG ALVAREZ

David Wolfberg
Julio Alvarez
Marcel Morlote
Joe Styrsky
Elvira Pita
Jorge Maldonado

COASTAL HOMES

Keith Sockaloski
John M. Murphy
John M. Murphy Jr.
Tom Murphy Sr.
Tom P. Murphy Jr.

TURNER CONSTRUCTION

Dan VonKossovsky
James Faria
Monty Taylor
Vito Verga
Roberto Gonzalez
Scott Digulimio
Eddie Arrazcaeta
Kelly Cantley
Ramon Troya
Scott Skidelsky
Jay Fraser

**DUANY PLATER-ZYBERK & COMPANY
MASTER PLAN AND
ARCHITECTURE DESIGN**

Elizabeth Plater-Zyberk
Ludwig Fontalvo-Abello
Xavier Iglesias

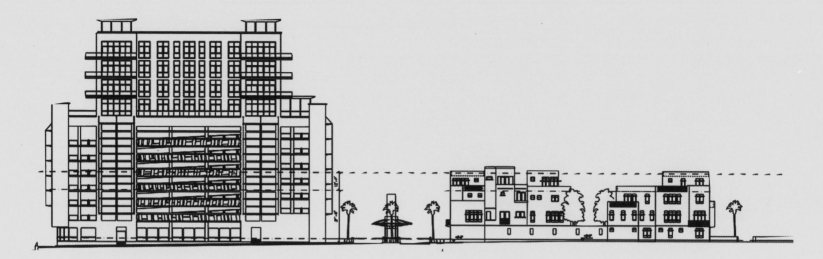

FROM 63RD STREET

ARI WAY NORTH AND SOUTH

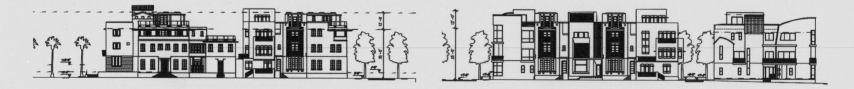

WATER WAY NORTH AND SOUTH